LITTLE RICHARD

The
BIRTH *of*
ROCK 'N' ROLL

LITTLE RICHARD

The
BIRTH *of*
ROCK 'N' ROLL

David Kirby

continuum

2009

The Continuum International Publishing Group Inc
80 Maiden Lane, New York, NY 10038

The Continuum International Publishing Group Ltd
The Tower Building, 11 York Road, London SE1 7NX

www.continuumbooks.com

A catalog record for this book is available from the Library of
Congress.

ISBN 978 0 82642 965 0

Typeset by Pindar NZ, Auckland, New Zealand
Printed in the United States of America

CONTENTS

"In the worst of times music is a promise that times are meant to be better."

— Robert Christgau

"Music's the only thing that makes sense any more, man."

— JoJo in Julie Taymor's film
Across the Universe

"Excitement wasn't in the air; it was the air."

— Greil Marcus,
The Rolling Stone History of Rock & Roll

"I am the only thing left."

— Little Richard

Introduction

I'm in Honolulu over Christmas break, stopping by Borders to get the *New York Times*, when I decide to slip upstairs to the music department and see what Little Richard CDs are on offer. There are none. Now I could have ordered whatever I wanted, but that wouldn't have changed the facts: an informed customer walks into a well-stocked music store in a good-sized city and fails, even after seeking help, to find a single CD by the King of Rock and Roll, the Man Who Started It All, the Georgia Peach, and now, in his own words, the Only Thing Left.

Maybe that's just Honolulu, though, where the languid heartbreak of a slack-key guitar solo might be expected to trump the take-no-prisoners aggression of piano boogie. But when I get home to Tallahassee, the same is true at the Borders there: plenty of Lita Ford and Living Colour, but no Little Richard between them.

So I take my quest for Richardiana to the Virgin

Megastore in Times Square. At last! Here I find assorted Little Richard CDs, five in all. Yet there are six by the Little River Band and a startling 29 by Little Feat. The Little River Band is best known for the cloying "Lady" and what is surely one of the worst of pop music's many celebrations of male self-pity, "Lonesome Loser." Little Feat is the better band. "Willin'," from their first album, is a beautiful song about missing somebody during a long night of driving under the influence of "weed, whites, and wine," though it was popularized by Linda Ronstadt rather than the band itself. But Little Feat is still little more than a pothole in rock's long and well-traveled highway.

I'm not sure how to read these numbers: is Little Feat that popular, or are there so many of their CDs because the store can't sell them?

Everywhere, Little Richard is nowhere. But sometimes that's how genius works. I once devoted an entire book with the ungainly title *Ultra-Talk: Johnny Cash, the Mafia, Shakespeare, Drum Music, St. Teresa Of Avila, and 17 Other Colossal Topics of Conversation* to the idea that nothing's good in art and life and culture unless it's embraced repeatedly by both an intellectual elite and the masses. Meanwhile, time has to work its slow, inexorable, and sometimes totally inept magic. Yeah, the best will out — usually. But sometimes it needs a little nudge.

That's where I figured all those great music writers out there would come to my aid. For every two CDs or vinyl LPs on my walls, there's at least one book by a writer I idolize or an article I've cut out or one that's gathering dust in a pile of magazines I haven't gotten to yet. Again and again, though, while these scholars and journalists seem to be aware of Little Richard, they don't have much to say about him. It's sort of like saying you're religious but you don't have anything to say about God.

And that's not a far-fetched analogy, because many of these writers treat Little Richard as though he were the Prime Mover.

For example, the preface of a book which takes its title from Richard's greatest song, Nik Cohn's *Awopbopaloobop Alopbamboom: The Golden Age of Rock*, brims with all the promise of the book's title. Growing up in the Protestant section of Derry in Ireland, Cohn writes that "one evening I'd gone astray, found myself on the fringes of Bogside, the Catholic slum. Across the street I heard Little Richard singing 'Tutti Frutti' on a coffee-bar jukebox. Watched the local teen hoods — Teddy Boys, they were called — with their duckass haircuts and drainpipe jeans, jiving in plain day. Had my first glimpse of sex, and danger, and secret magic. And I have never been healthy since." But while Cohn's book is named after (and its last words are) the hook of the song that changed his and everybody else's world, for crissakes, its chapters are devoted to Bill Haley, Elvis Presley, Eddie Cochran, the Beatles, the Stones . . . everybody but Little Richard, whom Cohn refers to as "a guaranteed genuine rock howler out of Macon, Georgia" as well as "the real thing" and the entertainer "who was and still is the most exciting live performer I ever saw in my life."

And that's it: a mention here, a compliment there, but

nothing about the man's indispensable contributions to the world we live in today.

And what are those contributions? In a nutshell, they come down to "Tutti Frutti," the one song that hit young Nik Cohn like a bolt from the blue. The subtitle of my book is really a co-title: all the parts that make up rock 'n' roll had been moving toward critical mass for years, but when Little Richard shouted, "A-wop-bop-a-loo-mop, a-lop-bam-boom," suddenly, to quote the Book of Genesis, there was a firmament in the midst of the waters. It's a huge song musically, but it's also a seminal text in American culture, as much as *Uncle Tom's Cabin*, "Song of Myself," and the great documents of the Civil Rights era are. In a sense, it's America's Other National Anthem.

Consider where "Tutti Frutti" came from. You can trace the roots of rock 'n' roll back to every branch on the musical tree, especially gospel, but to most people who were listening to the radio in 1955, rock's most immediate ancestors were pop and rhythm 'n' blues. Riffing on Carl Belz's definitions in *The Story of Rock*, I'd say pop is kitschy, easy-going and white, where r 'n' b is bluesy, loud and black — think Patti Page doing "How Much is That Doggie in the Window?" (1952) about the same time that Fats Domino was singing "Ain't That a Shame" (1955). Rock combines the two, according to Belz, taking its subject matter from pop and its style from rhythm 'n' blues, and here you might think of the Beatles' "She Loves You" (1963). Or "Tutti Frutti."

With its nonsense syllables, the song at the center of this book is a silly song, in many ways — certainly Pat

Boone tried to make his version of "Tutti Frutti" a totally pop treatment and thus a silly song in every way. Yet its rhythms give it urgency, and some of its lyrics even give it a sexual urgency (the gal named Sue "knows just what to do"). Art results when the deliberate is transformed by the accidental, and what begin deliberately in the New Orleans recording session that produced "Tutti Frutti" was transformed by a series of happy accidents I'll describe in detail in Chapter 3. All new music changes the world, but no music changed the world the way this song did. If it's at the center of this book, that's because it's at the center of our culture.

Why haven't more cultural historians realized this? Nik Cohn is not the only one to jump back like Moses after God handed him the Ten Commandments and say, "I don't think I want to go up on that mountain any more." You'd think a book with a title like William E. Studwell and D. F. Lonergan's *The Classic Rock and Roll Reader: Rock Music from Its Beginnings to the Mid-1970s* would give ample or at least adequate attention to the creator of rock 'n' roll or, at the very least, toss him and his music a paragraph or two. But no: "Tutti Frutti" is not listed under "Pioneering Rock Songs" or "Megastars and Megagroups" or even "Best Songs That Never Made Number 1." Instead, the song that changed music forever is in the "Novelty Songs" chapter along with Sammy Davis, Jr.'s silly "The Candy Man" as well as "Itsy Bitsy Teenie Weenie Yellow Polkadot Bikini," "The Purple People Eater," and others by Petula Clark, the Fifth Dimension and the David Seville who was responsible for the Alvin and the Chipmunk Records. Can you imagine? The rock howler out of Macon on the same plane as three musical rodents.

Another classic text, *The Story of Rock* mentioned above, was informed, helpful, and, in the end, disappointing because it, like most works of its kind, pays so little attention to the man who started it all. Little Richard is mentioned ten times, though almost always in a list including Chuck Berry, Fats Domino, Ray Charles and other pioneers. And "Tutti Frutti" is mentioned exactly once — as a song Pat Boone covered.

Little Richard, where are you? The answer is that he is right there in front of us where apparently we can't see him. On a June 2008 episode of *The Young and the Restless* that's available on YouTube, a couple wants to get married in Las Vegas by an impersonator. Liberace is their first choice, but he's suffering from food poisoning, so they go with Little Richard — the real Little Richard, as it turns out, but the couple can't tell.

And there's a chapter on Little Richard in Zell Miller's *They Heard Georgia Singing*, a guide to the many musicians the Peach State has produced, but he's not in the first place most people turn to in a reference book: the index. One wonders if Miller has an agenda here. After all, as the governor of Georgia, he became so sold on the then-popular idea that classical music improves brain development that he mandated the distribution of free copies of a Sony CD called *Build Your Baby's Brain Through the Power of Music* to new parents. So after Junior has been lulled by chestnuts like Pachelbel's

"Canon in D Major," does Mom really want him to pop out of his playpen like a piece of burnt toast when he hears a crazy guy shout "A-wop-bop-a-loo-mop, a-lop-bam-boom"?

And so it goes. After Greil Marcus, Peter Guralnick is my favorite music writer. As you'll see in the pages that follow, there's no way I can repay Guralnick for what I learned from *Sweet Soul Music* and his other books. So it's easy to imagine the eagerness with which I took up his *Feel Like Going Home: Portraits in Blues & Rock 'n' Roll* as well as my dismay when I read, on the first page, "I am sorry circumstances prevented me from including Little Richard or Chuck Berry." Wait — you're painting portraits of rock's Founding Fathers, but not Little Richard and Chuck?

The rock press isn't much better. The *Rolling Stone* issue immediately following the 2008 Grammy Awards covered the event in three different features: an analysis of the show's ratings (not high, in what the writer called "a divided musical culture"), a photo collection, and a column on dominant personalities that mentioned Alicia Keys, Kanye West, Kid Rock, Lil Wayne, Amy Winehouse and Cyndi Lauper — but not Jerry Lee Lewis and Little Richard, both of whom performed on the live broadcast. I'm sorry, Jann Wenner and company, but I've seen Kid Rock rock, and he's no Little Richard.

The one notable exception to the print media's neglect of Little Richard is the cover story of the June 2007 issue of the British magazine *Mojo*. The story is titled "100 Records That Changed the World." The magazine's cover depicts two lines of floating heads that converge in the center. The Beatles, Bob Marley and Mick Jagger are on one side, Elvis, James Brown and Aretha on the other. The lines meet in a full-figure representation of Little Richard looking like the love child of the Sacred Heart of Jesus and some Hindu temple goddess. Inside, the songs march from #100 to #1, through work by the Sex Pistols, Ray Charles, Robert Johnson, Bob Dylan.

And the list ends with the proclamation "In the Beginning was the Word" and goes on to explain that "the word was A-wop-bop-a-loo-mop-a-lop-bam-boom! A torrent of filth wailed by a bisexual alien, Little Richard's 'Tutti Frutti' smashed down the doors of culture and ushered in an attitude we still call rock 'n' roll." Later in the article, "Tutti Frutti" is described as "the biggest bang in the history of pop music."

So of all the mags out there, *Mojo* got Little Richard right. Otherwise, zip. But sometimes that's the way it is for the ones who matter most. As it says in the liner notes to the Robert Johnson album *King of the Delta Blues Singers*, "Robert Johnson appeared and disappeared, in much the same fashion as a sheet of newspaper twisting and twirling down a dark and windy midnight street." The bigger the profile, the harder it is to see. Who knows who Shakespeare is, or Jesus?

Also, Little Richard himself hasn't exactly stayed in one spot and made it easy for rock historians to shine on him the light of his own importance. Almost as soon as he became famous, he notoriously abandoned rock for gospel, and whenever he seemed on the verge of a comeback, he fled the arena yet again and holed up in church. And, as my own experiences with him will show, he remains maddeningly elusive, even to those who only want him to take his proper place on the cultural stage.

Nor has he tended his own legacy with much care. Joseph Johnson, curator of the Georgia Music Hall of Fame, told me he spent a week talking to Little Richard at the Hyatt on Hollywood's Sunset Strip and trying to get him to donate materials to the Hall's museum. At one point, the entertainer began to yank one typically outrageous costume after another off a room-long rack and toss them at Johnson, who said, "Wait, wait — I need to know when you wore this and where," to which Little Richard replied, "How would I know?" Nor had he saved any posters, flyers, photos, contracts: none of that. Johnson said that the country singer Travis Tritt, also a Hall of Fame inductee, had told him recently that he always walked through the airport with his cowboy hat in one hand and a briefcase full of business papers in the other. But like Oscar Wilde, when Little Richard goes through Customs, apparently he has nothing to declare but his talent.

As you might expect, the rockers Little Richard influenced know how much they owe him. Neil Young says, "Chuck Berry and Little Richard? That's rock and roll. That's the real shit. . . . When you listen to him now and you go back to those days, it's Jerry Lee and Little Richard. That's what it is. Elvis was comin' in a distant third when you get right down to it."

And interestingly, my 19- and 20-year-old students

often seemed to have a better idea of who Little Richard is and why he's important than the critics do. In the spring of 2008, I handed out a questionnaire to two groups of students asking basic questions. A couple of students weren't quite sure who he was or confused him with Chuck Berry or Bo Diddley, but most had a strong visual sense of the Little Richard persona, though they might have gotten that from the GEICO commercial (available on YouTube) as much as any other source. Most students associated him more with rock, soul or r 'n' b than pop. Many knew that he was responsible for what they described as the "revival of spirit in music," the "rebirth of piano playing," "a new style and sound" and "massive vocal screeches."

Oddly, though, in a way, accurately, two students described him as having a positive "post-Elvis" influence and reappropriating the blackness that was spirited away by the King — oddly, because Little Richard was already on the scene before Elvis's heyday; accurately, because the masses who were called back to their own bodies by Elvis's televised wrigglings later came to recognize rock's real pioneers. The best response to the question "How did he affect the music that followed his?" came from a student who wrote: "By being himself, he inspired thousands of others." That number's a little low, but to paraphrase the Who, the kid's all right.

I was heartened to see that my 2008 students knew that Little Richard was at least as important as a Founding Father as Elvis and probably more so. Twenty years earlier, I don't think my classes would have felt the same way. If I had asked students then who started rock, most would have said Elvis. True, Elvis became the King, but mainly because he was white and tamed by producers and thus sellable not only to the kids but also the parents who paid for their records. And as I'll argue later, while Elvis was gutted by management all too soon, he did perform one act that no one else could have, which is that, by wriggling until it looked as though his pants were about to fly off, he gave back to kids the bodies their parents, pastors and principals had tried to take away. (We'll overlook for the moment the impossibility of Little Richard or any other African American being permitted to bust a sexy move in the early days of network television.)

So it's not that I think white guys didn't contribute. In fact, for my money, the pure crazy manifestation of everything thrilling in rock 'n' roll is summed up in the person of Jerry Lee Lewis, described on the Rock and Roll Hall of Fame web site as "the wild man of rock and roll, embodying its most reckless and high-spirited impulses. On such piano-pounding rockers from the late Fifties as 'Whole Lotta Shakin' Goin' On' and 'Great Balls of Fire,' Lewis combined a ferocious, boogie-style instrumental style with rowdy, uninhibited vocals."

Jerry Lee said this of Elvis: "Elvis was my friend and you'd better believe it. Elvis Presley loved Jerry Lee Lewis. Elvis was a good person — we had a good time together. We were two of the same kind." But then he added, "Elvis opened the door, man, but he couldn't follow Jerry Lee on stage — no siree." I've seen the Killer tear up more than one concert hall, and he's right about that.

Of course, you could also argue that the Prime Mover of rock is Chuck Berry, of whom it is said on the Rock Hall web site, "While no individual can be said to have invented rock and roll, Chuck Berry comes the closest of any single figure to being the one who put all the essential pieces together." Or, as John Lennon said, "If you tried to give rock and roll another name, you might call it 'Chuck Berry.'"

And let's not forget Fats Domino, who said, "Well, I wouldn't want to say that I started it, but I don't remember anyone else before me playing that kind of stuff." And even Elvis admitted, "Let's face it: I can't sing it like Fats Domino can. I know that."

There was a tribute concert to Fats in New York in 2007 as well as an album with songs by Tom Petty, Neil Young, Norah Jones, Lucinda Williams, B. B. King, Willie Nelson and Robert Plant, among others. Now there was a Hurricane Katrina tie-in; for a while, the Fat Man was thought to have perished in the storm along with nearly 2,000 others as George W. Bush's government looked the other way, and both concert and album raised funds for the hurricane's victims.

Still, where's the Little Richard tribute? Sir Paul McCartney played on the Fats Domino album; you'd think he'd do the same for a musician whose songs he and the other boys from Liverpool opened their shows with and who influenced the Beatles more than anyone else.

Okay, maybe I'm being too hard on public opinion here. True, Little Richard doesn't writhe like Elvis on TV.

Nor can he play or write songs like Chuck or channel Satan on stage like Jerry Lee or sell sweetness the way Fats does.

But to paraphrase Isaiah Berlin (who himself borrowed from the Greek poet Archilochus), the world is divided into foxes and hedgehogs; the fox does many things, and the hedgehog does one Big Thing. And Little Richard's Big Thing is that, under extraordinary circumstances that will be recounted in detail in Chapter 3 of this book, on the afternoon of September 14, 1955, he recorded a song called "Tutti Frutti." From start to finish, the song lasts 2 minutes and 25 seconds, yet, in the words of Keith Richards, it was as if, in a single instant, the world changed from monochrome to Technicolor.

"Much has been written about the transition of rhythm and blues into rock 'n' roll, the term coined by disc jockey Alan Freed to describe the irrepressible music that caught the fancy of white teenagers in the middle fifties," write Grace Lichtenstein and Laura Dankner. "But the transition was summed up best during a session at the J & M studio, when a flamboyant gay black pianist from Georgia sang ten syllables that shook the world."

What was the first rock 'n' roll song? Candidates abound, from Wynonie Harris's "Good Rockin' Tonight" to Bill Haley's "Rock Around the Clock" and Elvis's "That's All Right (Mama)." There's an entire book devoted to the subject, Jim Dawson and Steve Propes's *What Was the First Rock 'n' Roll Record?*, though the authors don't reach a definitive conclusion. Probably the best advice is to do what Jim and Doug Oade of Oade Brothers Audio in

Thomasville, Georgia told me in one of my interviews with them: when in doubt, trust your ears. If you do that, you just may agree that no song has had the impact of "Tutti Frutti" on fans and musicians alike, and no other song has flooded the world with so much bright color.

Or so says Keith Richards. What I say is this: for centuries, everything in human history churned slowly towards Cosimo Matassa's tiny recording studio in New Orleans on that fateful day in the middle of the century. There, all we know on earth and all we need to know about love, freedom, desire and the need to boogie come together for less than 3 minutes. Then out of this brief moment flows everything we know and want and ever will, just as the lives we're living came from a cosmic bang that was as powerful as it was brief. In shaping this book, I've replicated that pattern: its middle chapter, the one on "Tutti Frutti," is the shortest, and in this way it divides the world into two eras, the one that came before that song and the one you live in now.

I want Little Richard to be seen for who he is. Long before I even thought about writing a book like this, I wrote "I hear America singing, and it sounds like Little Richard." This is in the title poem of a book called *The House of Blue Light*, in which I say Little Richard is not just a singer. To me, he's a way of looking at the world.

Now I get to make good on that premise in this book. "Tutti Frutti" occupies a finite space smack in the middle of our huge-ass Crab Nebula of a culture. It's like the skinniest part of an hourglass: everything that came before flows into this narrow pass, and the world we live in today flows out the other side. The world was one color, and now it's every color. Little Richard seems to be tugging on the robe of the God he worships when he says "I am the only thing left," but he's right.

The method I use here is similar to one I have used in my other non-fiction books. I began by reading everything that has been written about my subject, listening to every available recording, and visiting the places and talking to the people most closely connected to him; as Charles Nicholl says in his biography *The Lodger Shakespeare*, "We are in search of facts but we also listen to the whispers." After that, I did my best to write a compelling narrative, one that has the sweep of history as well as the immediacy of a newspaper headline.

Chapter 1 will portray Little Richard in the days before his showbiz career, and here the emphasis is on a magical place called Macon, a place I call Everybody's Other Home Town. The second chapter will continue the story of the Macon days but in the context of that invisible republic that Greil Marcus calls the Old, Weird America and the songs that rise from it like mist in a moonlit swamp. The third and shortest chapter concentrates on "Tutti Frutti," after which the book opens out again. Chapter 4 treats Little Richard's impact on the then-new teen culture that has shaped the world we live in now, and the fifth and final chapter describes his place in history and his present-day profile as established by the showbiz template he created, the stories his intimates tell, his movie roles and his still-sizzling concerts. His appearances in movies have never been examined in detail, and

I do so here because, for the generations that didn't grow up with him, film is the best way to show his (and the world's) long, strange climb out of a segregated past and into a more enlightened day.

In the course of his career, Little Richard and associates — the women and men who co-wrote songs with him, his producers and fellow musicians — put on a clinic in songwriting, showing how the words are put together and the music made to support or slide by them. That process, too, is examined here. No one can teach you how to write a masterpiece, but anyone can learn from a close look at a songwriting process that changed music forever.

I met a woman in Charlottesville, Virginia recently who didn't know who Little Richard was, but she's the only one. On the other hand, I've met a lot of people who think they know who Little Richard is, but beyond a few songs and a sense of what he looks like, they might not know much more than the Charlottesville woman. What I'm doing here is not telling the story of his life again — the Charles White biography already does that job well — but describing the world before "Tutti Frutti" and then after, a world in which we no longer see race or religion or sex or business or entertainment or our own daily lives in the same way, and all because of one 2-minute-and-25-second song.

In a perfect world, *Little Richard: The Birth of Rock 'n' Roll* would be the pool cue that bounces the eight ball of the singer and his songs off every cushion in the reader's mind before it sinks into the corner pocket of his or her heart. That's asking a little too much, though, given how widely musical tastes vary. But at least I can give Little Richard the place in history he deserves. Writing in the magazine *Wavelength*, Rick Coleman calls "Tutti Frutti" the Big Bang from which everything else emanated, and Charles White calls Little Richard the Quasar of Rock 'n' Roll. Now a quasar is among the most distant yet luminous bodies in the universe, an extremely old celestial object whose power output is nonetheless several thousand times that of our present galaxy. If you love pop or rock or hip-hop or just about any kind of music that's out there today, Little Richard is the reason why.

And if you think the best world is one in which black folks and white ones live and work together and learn from each other along with Hispanics and Asians and Arabs and peoples of every race, creed and color, well, Little Richard's behind that, too. In addition to the other nicknames he has, he should also be called the Integrator.

If this book were a car, let's put it this way: it wouldn't be one of those little three-wheeled numbers that are just right for European streets, or even a Volkswagen bug. Nor would it be a hybrid or any car of recent vintage, for that matter, the kind that's all computers, that you can't crawl under the hood of and work on with a set of socket wrenches. It'd be a hooptie — an Oldsmobile 88, say. As it came from the factory, the 88 was a pretty solid car, good enough to be immortalized in Ike Turner's 1951 "Rocket 88," a 12-bar blues credited to Jackie Brenston and his Delta Cats, a band that didn't exist (the song was recorded by Turner's Kings of Rhythm, one of whom was saxophonist Jackie Brenston). The 88 was also a 25-foot-long German anti-tank gun that fired 88 mm rounds over a 6-mile distance and scared the bejeezus out of the Brits during the desert war; like Little Richard, it made a hell of a lot of noise. Eighty-eight is also the number of keys on Little Richard's instrument of choice, as well as the exact amount of money he made me pull out of my wallet the first time I spoke with him (more on that in Chapter 1).

But this Olds would have gone through a lot of customizing. The chassis is by Charles White, whose *The Life and Times of Little Richard: The Authorised Biography* may be superseded by another life some day, though not a better one. Actually, the *Life and Times* is an autobiography of sorts. White provides the embroidery that connects the sections, but most of the book consists of recollections by the Georgia Peach himself, making it a one-of-a-kind resource that rings not only with the facts of the speaker's life, which he reveals with a startling lack of self-consciousness, but also with Little Richard's greatest strength, which is his idiom. After all, it ain't what you do, as he sings in one of his songs, it's the way how you do it.

In fact, if there's any flaw in White's approach that I've tried to correct here it's that, by letting the singer have free rein and not shaping the material interpretatively, White is likely to leave the impression that Little Richard's greatest accomplishment is that he is the world's craziest nut. Then again, the original version of his book dates from 1984, when it may have been too soon to see what a world-changer Little Richard is. Still, the debt I and all fans owe Charles White is immense. His book doesn't figure on every page of mine or even in every chapter, but if I'm driving this thing and you're going along for the ride, suffice it to say that *The Life and Times of Little Richard* is there between you and me and the road.

And that's just the chassis. The design is by Greil Marcus, the rock critic who shows you how much you can get out of the music if you're willing to stray beyond the notes. His 1998 book *Invisible Republic: Bob Dylan's Basement Tapes* was published three years later under the more accurate title *The Old, Weird America*. That America, the one of medicine shows and bootleggers and itinerant bluesmen trying to stay one step ahead of the sheriff, is the one that Little Richard grew up in, that shaped his stage act and his songs, and that is still alive today, if you know where to look for it. (I do, and I'll tell you.) I rely on *The Old, Weird America* and other such masterful books by Marcus as *Mystery Train* and *Lipstick Traces* as I argue, like him, that every culture has two histories: the public one that's contained in official documents and the secret history that can be glimpsed in song lyrics and movies but also jokes and tall tales, not to mention the things people say to each other on street corners at night and the sound a train makes as it takes your baby to another town.

Then there's the upholstery in this car as well as (the pun is unavoidable) the headliner. Before the ink dried on the contract for this book, everything that makes up the world we occupy began to flow into it. Race, gender, sexuality, history, family dynamics, commerce, technology, art of every kind: every discipline in the curriculum carpeted the floors of this vehicle, covered its seats, lined its ceiling. Music is the main thing here, but it's not the only thing.

As far as the fuel I used to push this project along, that's easy. I filled the tank with Little Richard's music, of course, but also his high-octane live performances, film and video appearances, interviews, conversations. The first time I heard Little Richard's actual voice, I was in a room with his cousin in Macon when he called from Baltimore, and take my word for it: the phone wasn't necessary. The way Little Richard was yelling, he might as well have just stuck his head out the window in a city 600 miles to the north and saved on the toll charges. Hear his voice once, and you'll hear it forever; if you need help in that department, then for my money I'd say get the 1994 *Little Richard — Greatest Hits Recorded Live*, which captures a galvanic stage performance at the Okeh Club in Hollywood, California. I myself have heard Little Richard's voice above the roar of the NASCAR track at Talladega and under the stillness of a Trappist monastery in Kentucky: I hear America singing, indeed. I hope you hear that voice in these pages.

Finally, there are all the appointments, all the chrome and glass, yeah, but also the knobs and buttons that turn on the engine and the lights and the radio and make everything work. These bits and pieces come from all over that great parts warehouse that is the USA, but mainly from its Macon branch. It was there that I met Ruth Sykes of the Macon-Bibb County Convention and Visitors Bureau, who made it possible for me to interview Willie Ruth Howard, Little Richard's cousin, as well as Karla Redding-Andrews, Otis Redding's daughter, and Zelma Redding, his widow. Ruth also put me on to a great ball of fire, Lisa Love, executive director of the Georgia Music Hall of Fame, and her sidekick, Joseph Johnson, the Hall's curator and himself an archive of music lore.

Kenneth Rollins of the Douglass Theatre, where Otis, Richard, James Brown and dozens of others in the rich Middle Georgia music scene got their start, introduced me to Newton Collier, former trombone player for Sam and Dave, companion on many a club crawl and my secret weapon as I pierced the veil to see what was really going on in Macon past and present. Legendary DJ Hamp Swain filled me in on the early days of Little Richard as an entertainer when he performed with Hamp's band, the Hamptones. Seaborn Jones, poet and man of parts, paints a portrait of Little Richard unlike any other; thanks to Seaborn, I got to know a man few do. Alan Walden, who, with his brother Phil, is an indelible part of music history, is a mesmerizing raconteur; his wife, Tosha, and daughters, Jessica and Georgeanna, get points for making sure that Alan stopped fishing long enough to tell me his stories of the old days and the ones to come.

Many of those I interviewed for this book are in their 70s or older, which lent urgency to my enterprise: I wanted to get their stories while they were still around to tell them. Generally, I've found that while stars are unapproachable — fans bore them, for the most part, and stalkers frighten them — the people who knew and worked with them are right there in the phone book and eager to talk. So you can't pick up the phone and talk to Little Richard, but you can call Cosimo Matassa in New Orleans, and he'll tell you what happened on September 14, 1955, when he recorded "Tutti Frutti" in a cramped studio on Rampart Street in New Orleans. Phil "Pee Wee" Clark, who played steel guitar with Uncle Ned and the Hayloft Jamboree in Macon and now lives in Brisbane, Australia, has a fistful of Little Richard stories, as does owner Chuck Howard and bartender Leroy of the now defunct Jazz Plex club; so does Tommy Barnes, whom I bumped into at the Tic Toc Room, where Little Richard used to sing when it was known as Ann's Tick-Tock Club, and whose parents went to school with the performer. Historian Cameron Pennybacker sent me books and schooled me in the dark days of Macon's racial history.

Beth and Elliott Dunwody of Bright Blue Sky Productions showed me old videos and opened other doors for me. Maconites Judson Mitcham, Phil Comer and Rob Apsley egged me on; field recording geniuses Jim and Doug Oade explained the technical side of things more than once and taught me that, as far as technology goes, the only rule is "trust your ears." Willie Ruth Howard's grandson, Vincent Harrison, preached the gospel to me when I was visiting her and pointed out that, like Little Richard, Jesus, too, came from a small town.

My masters at various journals and newspapers have made it possible for me to publish parts of this book as I went along and even pick up an occasional check to help with expenses. David Kelly of the *New York Times Book Review* sends me wonderful music books to review; music critics Jon Pareles and Ben Ratliff of the *Times* have offered answers and encouragement. Ann Maloney and especially Keith Spera of the *New Orleans Times-Picayune* put me in touch with key figures from the music scene in the Crescent City, where "Tutti Frutti" was recorded. K. C. Summers, travel editor of the *Washington Post*, commissioned a piece called "Good Golly! It's Macon Music" that served as an entree to life in that town like no other. Reid Davis, editor of *Georgia Music*, gives me yummy assignments on Little Richard and other key figures in the Georgia scene, and Susan Hahn of *TriQuarterly* has let me write as much as I want about rock in general and Little Richard in particular.

My Florida State colleague Barry Faulk is a two-legged encyclopedia of music and someone I always learn from, as are Robert Olen Butler, Leigh Edwards, Scott Kopel and Mark Winegardner. Rip Lhamon is the author of *Deliberate Speed: The Origins of a Cultural Style in the American 1950s*, a book to which anyone who has written about this period is indebted, as am I. Mac Craig is one of the many people who told me about something I didn't know existed; in Mac's case, it's the episode of the *Bill and Ted's Excellent Adventures* cartoon series in which Mozart time travels to Macon to jump-start Little Richard's career. My sons, Ian and Will, constantly bring me up to date on today's music and the changing ways in which it's delivered.

My wife, Barbara Hamby, is a writer as well, and she loves words and music of all kinds as much as I do. I've had to jump down more than one rabbit hole as I wrote this book, and she's always there when I pop back to the surface. There are Pentecostals and moonshiners in her family tree. Her grandfather is said to have been strangled by her grandmother's brothers, and some think the old lady herself was in on it; the coroner's verdict was heart attack, but the first person to see his body said Grandpa had "grape jelly stains" around his neck.

As I look back over these words of thanks, I see that I have written about a song recorded by a band that doesn't exist, a biography that's actually an autobiography, a book about historical uncertainty that can't make up its mind what its own title is, an America that's there and isn't, an elegant woman whose great-uncles Taft and Mockingbird (real name: Elijah) may have killed their brother in law — the jury's still out on that one — though it's certain that Mockingbird had a vision of sinners in the pit that put an end to his carousing and started him on a godly path, all in the course of a single tortured night.

These are my car's parts, and they're welded together with the solder of accidental conversation, like the machine in Johnny Cash's "One Piece at a Time" that's smuggled off a Detroit assembly line and put together bit by bit until it emerges as a full-blown psychobilly Cadillac. This is a handmade book, in other words, and its subject is a handmade world, one that doesn't exist anymore, that doesn't exist yet. Birth and death are still primitive. We're born into the Old, Weird America and we die into it. Nightly, we visit it in our dreams. In that country, Little Richard's both the champ and the chump, the diva and the dishwasher, but then so are you, reader, and so am I. The Old, Weird America came into being when you turned the car radio on in 1955 and heard somebody say "A-wop-bop-a-loo-mop, a-lop-bam-boom!" Two minutes and 25 seconds later, the sound stops as abruptly as though you've gone off the road and hit a tree; you look at the calendar, and it's 2009.

Let's take a ride.

CHAPTER 1

Early One Morning

"What are you doing in my cousin's apartment?" says Little Richard, and the answer is that I've come to Macon to write a travel piece for the *Washington Post* and also do research for a book on the Georgia Peach himself. Willie Ruth Howard is two years older than her celebrated relative, which makes her 77, and even though it's a hot day, I've put on a sports coat and brought flowers, too, because I want her to think I'm a gentleman and not just a fan trying to hop aboard the singer's coattails.

When the phone rings, she talks for a minute and says, "It's him," and "He wants to talk to you," but before I can start telling Little Richard how the world changed for me when I turned on my little green plastic Westinghouse radio in 1955 and heard a voice say, "A-wop-bop-a-loo-mop, a-lop-bam-boom!" he says, "What are you doing in my cousin's apartment?" and then "Uh-huh. Well, look around you. You can see that my cousin is very poor, can't you?" and I'm thinking, well, she looks as though she's doing okay to me, but who am I to disagree with Little Richard, so I say, "Sure — yeah!" and he says, "Well, then, what I want you to do is get out your checkbook and write her a check for five hundred dollahs!" and I'm thinking, Jeez, I brought her these flowers. . . .

But then I say, "Mr. Richard, I mean, Mr. Penniman, I don't have my checkbook with me," which is true, and I also want to say, "Wait, who's the wealthy rock star here, you or me?" But mainly I don't want him to hang up, and I'd been to the ATM the night before, so I say, "I do have $100 in my wallet," and he says, "Okay, get your wallet out," and I say, "It's out," and he says, "Now take the money out," and I do, which is when I realize that I'd gone to a club last night after I'd hit the ATM, so now I only have $88, and I tell him that, and he says, "Okay, put it on the coffee table," so I put my bills on the coffee table, and he says, "Where's the money now?" and I say, "On the coffee table!" and he says, "Now tell Willie Ruth to get her purse," so I say, "Willie Ruth, Little Richard wants you to get your purse," so she says, "Okay!"

So Willie Ruth disappears into the other room and comes back with the purse, and I say, "She's back," and he says, "Now give her the phone," and I do, and from where I'm sitting — this is Little Richard, after all — I hear him say, "Put the money in your purse!" and she says "Okay!" and he says, "Where is the money now?" and she says, "In the purse!" and he says, "Okay, now take the purse back into the other room," and she does, and when she comes back, he says, "Now give the phone back to him," so Willie Ruth passes me the phone, and he says, "Where's the money?" and I say, "It's in Willie Ruth's purse, which is in the other room," and he says, "Thank you!" And I say, "You're welcome, Mr. Penniman! But I'd really like to talk to you as well, so how do you feel about giving me your phone number?" and he says, "I'm not at home right now! I'm in Baltimore!" and I say, "That's good, but can I call you when you're back in Tennessee, maybe fly up and see you some time?" and he says, "I'm not in Tennessee! I told you — I'm in Baltimore!" and I say, "I know, but when you *are* in Tennessee," but he says, "Give her the phone again!" and while Willie Ruth is ending the call, I'm looking around and thinking, did Little Richard just get me to take $88 out of my wallet and give it to a cousin I've barely met?

I feel like a jerk. I think, 88 is the number of keys on a piano, like the instrument referred to by the Capitols in their 1961 r 'n' b chart topper "Cool Jerk" when they say, "Now give me a little bit of bass with those 88s." At the moment, though, I have the 88 dollar blues. I could write a song about it: "I have the 88 dollar blues / I've been plundered. / I say I have the 88 dollar blues / yes, I'm plundered. / Little Richard fired a round into my travel expenses / but at least it wasn't five hunnerd."

On the other hand, I've probably spent more than that on a single phone call to some woman I was breaking up with, and a fairly horrible woman, too, or else she'd be with me today. My goodness! How'd that be, to be chained to a shrew who despised me and treated me like her servant, an attitude hardly calculated to improve my disposition, so that I, in turn, would become more and more truculent and pettish and in that way increase her disdain for me. . . . When I look up, the call's over, and Willie Ruth is sitting quietly on the couch with the phone in her hand, and she says, "Was he rude?" and I say, "Uh . . . business-like!"

Which is true, because while he was forceful and direct, he wasn't discourteous. And I didn't have to part with a cent, but I did, and now I'm talking to Willie Ruth Howard, and she's saying, "Well, you know, he did get cheated a lot back when he was first starting out, when those record company people took all the money and didn't leave the singers with anything. Besides, he was so poor growing up. So poor. . . ."

"My mama had 12 children, and we were pretty but we were poor," as Little Richard said at a recent concert in New York. "All that beauty, and wasn't nobody on duty. All that honey and no money." He was born December 5, 1932, one of the 12 children of Charles "Bud" Penniman, a Seventh Day Adventist preacher who owned a bar called the Tip In Inn and sold moonshine on the side, and Leva Mae Penniman, just 14 when she married.

And already, at the very moment he enters the world, the Little Richard story takes a turn toward the unreliable. For the name on his birth certificate reads Richard Wayne Penniman, but Leva Mae says he was named Ricardo Wayne; nobody ever bothered to straighten out the mix-up. His right leg was also shorter than his left, and there were other abnormalities, at least from his perspective: "I had this great big head and little body," he recalls in Charles White's biography, "and I had one big eye and one little eye."

He had size, too, at least at the beginning. "He was the biggest baby I ever had," Leva Mae remembers, "ten pounds at birth." In person, the adult Little Richard doesn't look as though he started life in double digits. His personality has always been king-sized, though, and no doubt some who knew him as a child in Macon may have wished it smaller.

Take Miz Ola. "I had a bowel movement in a box, a shoebox or something like that," Little Richard remembers, "and I packed it up like a present and gave it to an old lady next to Mathis Groceries, on Monroe Street, in Pleasant Hill." It was Miz Ola's birthday, and she had some friends over, so young Richard waited around the corner to see what would happen next. Naturally everybody wanted to see what the cute neighborhood boy had brought, but the next thing he hears is "Aaaaaaa, aaaaaahhh — I'm gonna kill him!" Though a cripple, Miz Ola dropped her stick and leapt off the porch to murder the mischievous child. It was Little Richard's first miracle, and he escaped to perform many others.

As he tells Charles White, Richard went on to do his "no-manners" in other jars and boxes and leave them for his mother to find, and readers fascinated with that aspect of his early life will find the details in the biography. But the Miz Ola incident says a lot about the once and future rock star. On my first visit to Macon, I was appalled by how run-down Little Richard's neighborhood was, and this after 70 years of "improvement" — at least today the streets are paved.

But the house his family lived in is on the verge of dilapidation; there's no question of its being preserved as a historical site. There's a satellite dish on a side wall and an air conditioning unit hanging out of one window, but the screen on the front porch is torn and hanging; all it needs is a latter-day Little Richard to pull it away and crawl in, maybe do his no-manners on the door step and leave it for a hapless renter to find.

Locals tell me that the house is slated to be pulled down soon to make way for an off-ramp on I-75, which runs nearly overhead. The only reason the house hasn't been vandalized is the presence of Gary, a house painter who was the historic spot's temporary resident. Tired and spattered after a long day's work, Gary welcomed a nosy writer in and let him poke around.

"You know who lived here, don't you?" I ask, and Gary says, "Sure, I do." Going for a little of the Old, Weird America feel, I say, "I don't suppose you feel any, you know . . . vibrations?" The hair stands up on the back of my arms when Gary says, "Oh, all the time." "You do?" I gasp. "For real," says Gary as he sighs and jerks his thumb toward the interstate. "Dump trucks, semis, even the little cars: I feel 'em all."

Since those aren't exactly the kind of vibrations I mean, I reload and try again. "Well, is there anything in the house that you found that you could connect with Little Richard?" I ask. "Oh, there was a pitcher, but I throwed it away?" "A picture?" I say. "Yeah, it was one of them arty-graphs."

Inside, the more permanent fixtures looked worn and original, like the chipped bathtub in which Gary was soaking his work clothes and where Leva Mae bathed little Richard and his 11 boisterous and no doubt equally grimy siblings on all those sweaty Macon evenings when air conditioning was something only rich folks had.

It was a house in a neighborhood, in other words, where misbehavior might be a form of wealth, where a poor boy could lay up considerable emotional capital through the exercise of his imagination. Forget skin color for a minute and think *The Adventures of Tom Sawyer* and its celebrated sequel; in these books, the humorless Huck Finn is the good boy with a nascent sense of morality, and Tom is the one the other rascals admire, the magician who turns a Sunday School picnic into an Arab caravan and even stage-manages his own funeral. Yet Tom gets away with it, just as young Richard wasn't simply scandalizing the neighborhood ladies but, like Mark Twain's hero, beguiling them and avoiding punishment. To a boy with nothing, the ability to outrage and charm is as good as money.

And a boy like Little Richard needed all the resources he could muster. For one thing, he was a cripple; one leg was noticeably shorter than the other. When I saw him at his October 20, 2007 concert in St. Augustine, Little Richard said he went hip, hop, hip, hop when he walked: "I invented hiphop!" he cried. But high spirits are easy to come by late in life; in the kid-dominated world of boyhood Macon, he was teased without mercy, and he felt the sting.

His limp connected him to a side of life that the young Richard wasn't aware of yet. As his walk looked feminine, "the kids would call me faggot, sissy, freak, punk. They called me everything," he recalled. If his own witness is to be believed, Richard was soon having sex with women and men, and by his teen years, he had found a place in Macon's gay underworld.

This meant a break with two parts of his life that were really one, family and church. As a child, Richard performed with two gospel groups, the Tiny Tots and the family's Penniman Singers and appeared on stage at the Macon City Auditorium with the dynamic gospel pioneer Sister Rosetta Tharpe, from whom he learned more than one show-biz trick that he'd use later. He even thought about becoming a preacher himself.

Hormones and the lure of Macon's wild side took care of that impulse, at least for the moment, but it's impossible to underestimate the importance of the church on rock 'n' roll. When Maconites aren't telling you it's the water that's responsible for all the musical artistry in their town, they'll tell you the real source is the church. After all, a four-year-old boy is not going to hang a guitar around his neck and buy mikes and amps and recruit a drummer and a piano player and a horn section and schedule rehearsals and book gigs. But with some innate ability and a little bit of coaching, a child still in short pants can perform a solo on any Sunday morning. He can step up and sing and have the grownups beam down at him and pat his head, and when the service is over, he'll have somebody bring him a plate of chicken and greens and cornbread and a glass of sweet tea and tell him how handsome he is and how well he sang.

And that kind of reinforcement and nurturing can go on for years, at least until that boy decides that he's going to have more fun hanging around the Greyhound station at night and running with other young men who are discovering that they like a kind of sex that's not talked about in church. But by then, he knows the basics: how to form a group, for starters. How to blend the various sections of the choir into a harmony as well as when and how to introduce discord. How solos fit in, what audiences like, the way voice combines with instrument: all of these are things the choirboy sees and feels in every practice session, and then he sees how they all come together on Sunday morning.

Mainly, that boy learns how to put on a show: how a performance is set up, how it's sustained and then reaches a crescendo, and the many ways it can end, the best of which is when the whole choir stops at once and sits as though the members share a single behind, leaving the audience crying out for more, more, more. Charles White recalls a concert that ended when Little Richard jumped on top of his piano, tore his clothes off, threw them into the crowd, and disappeared, saying it was like having your throat cut in the middle of an orgasm. Anybody who's ever been to a full-tilt evangelical church service where the walls are shaking and everybody's high on Jesus knows where that moment comes from. You got to serve somebody, as Dylan says, and whether it's the devil or the Lord, the prayers are the same.

Periodically throughout his career, Little Richard abandoned rock 'n' roll and returned to gospel; now he blends the two in performance, playing hits by himself and others of his generation but interrupting himself in mid-song to praise the Lord and urging the audience between numbers to "not put a question mark where God has put a period." The battle of the sacred and profane is a Hundred Years' War of sorts among rock pioneers. As Nick Tosches recounts, there's no stronger evidence of the conflict's intensity than the recordings of Jerry Lee Lewis's drunken denunciations of the devil's music during the Sun Records recording of "Great Balls of Fire" where he explodes when producer Sam Phillips tries to suggest that rock 'n' roll might save certain sinners and the Killer shouts, "How can the, how can the *Devil* save souls? What are you talkin' about?"

More than one analyst has made the mistake of seeing this struggle as little more than a Jacob-and-the-angel wrestling match in which an individual is trying to salvage his own soul. But the stakes are a lot bigger than that.

Oppressed cultures have always turned to magic in one form or another as an answer to the no-exit tedium of their daily lives. It's no surprise to see the popularity of witchcraft peaking during the Middle Ages, when a punishing caste system locked you and yours into a round of endless labor and slow starvation while the guy on the hill trotted by on a fine charger caparisoned in sumptuous fabrics. If that were your lot, wouldn't you want to pull off your rags and dance around a campfire, shouting for Beelzebub? In Macon, there was plenty of witchcraft, on which more later. But the church, too, acted as a powerful antidote to widespread social ills.

"See, there was so much poverty, so much prejudice in those days," says Little Richard, so "people had to sing to feel their connection with God. To sing their trials away, sing their problems away, to make their burdens easier and the load lighter. That's the beginning. That's where it started." One constant in the singer's late life is his love for all things Macon, all things from his childhood, really — his family, the church, the town itself — every institution that kept him safe in his own mind in a time of want and chaos. So when Little Richard's performing on stage, for him to stop and glorify God in the middle of "Long Tall Sally" is not a kind of cramming for finals in which he's saving his soul so much as it is a move in the opposite direction, back to a past that is now changeless for him and that comforts like no other balm.

Of course, there was music other than the churchy kind in Richard's early life. There was the melody of daily life; like the Sam Cooke who let nothing go by and who made songs out of the groans of a chain gang and the excited cry of a nephew who shouted "Everybody cha-cha-cha!," Little Richard, too, had a sponge-like affinity to absorb and transmute the cries and chants he heard in the lanes of Macon. In the book that accompanies the three-disc Specialty Sessions of his recordings, the singer describes a man who used to beat a washboard and shout "a-bam-a-lam-bam" that sounds an awful lot like the seed of the famous cry that kicks off "Tutti Frutti." The child Richard also remembered a vegetable peddler with a horse and wagon who becomes a "little old man with a billy goat cart" in the indelible portrait painted by the mature Richard in "I Got It," an infectious ode to down-home living and the good eats that go with it.

Meanwhile, professional performers of all sorts helped the would-be entertainer who'd been raised on the music of his local church and neighborhood take a giant step forward. Brother Joe May, for example, a singing evangelist called the Thunderbolt of the West, would pass through on tour and leave an ambitious kid with an even stronger love of the spotlight. On the secular side, there was Billy Wright, "an entertainer that wore very loud-colored clothin', and shoethin'[sic] to match his clothin', and he wore his hair curled," Little Richard tells Charles White. "He influenced me a lot. He really enthused my whole life. I thought he was the most fantastic entertainer I had ever seen." Richard ended up joining Wright's band, as a matter of fact, and never stopped idolizing him. ("I really looked up to Billy Wright. That's where I got the hairstyle from and everything.")

It's impossible to be too outrageous, however, and where Wright's flamboyance ends, that of Esquerita begins. In the White biography, Little Richard mentions Esquerita in passing, remembering his real name as "SQ Rita" or "S. Q. Reeder", and says the flamboyant performer used to joke about his name in a no-manners way ("you know, excreta!"). But the Wikipedia article on Esquerita identifies him as Eskew Reeder, Jr., making his exotic soubriquet no more than a phonetic version of his square-sounding real name. He was born in Greenville, South Carolina, on November 20, 1935, and lived across the street from the young Jesse Jackson in the Greasy Corner community. Reeder attended Sterling High School from which Jackson graduated in 1959. He was basically a self-taught pianist and was accomplished enough to be playing in E. W. Watson's Tabernacle Baptist Church by the age of nine or ten. In his late teens, he dropped out of high school to join a gospel group based in New York called the Heavenly Echoes. In 1958, Reeder adopted the name "Esquerita" as part of a stage act that included heavy makeup and two wigs; in an internet photo, his 'do appears to be piled even higher than Little Richard's.

As a college student, I saw Esquerita and his band, the Eskerettes, play once at a Lambda Chi party. If you've seen *Animal House* and remember Otis Day and the Knights, who put on a minstrel show for the college boys and their dates, then you have the setting for the scene I'm about to describe. Born along one of the lighter branches of a stout Saxon oak, I'm still the whitest guy at just about any gathering, and, at 20, I was a pink-skinned blond whose hair flopped over a face rounded by cheeseburgers and Dixie beer. Little wonder that, halfway through a set of extended versions of grindhouse rousers like "Reelin' and Rockin'" and "My Ding-a-Ling," Esquerita scanned the audience, popped his wrist in my direction and, looking a lot more like a gay black Uncle Sam than the God in Michelangelo's Sistine Chapel fresco, said, "I want you!" as he waved me toward the stage.

On almost any other night, I would have been up there. But at the time I was dating, not a girl from a prominent family, but one whose family had pretensions. We split up after a while, but for the moment I was going along with her folks' fantasies of Caddies and McMansions instead of Chevy trucks and A-frames and staying away from anything even remotely scandalous. So I made vigorous not-me gestures as I backpedaled to a safe spot at the edge of the dance floor, whence I watched one of the brothers take the place that should have been mine. Pride and shame whipped across the chump's face as Esquerita popped the buttons on his Oxford shirt and lowered his khakis, and as he stood there abashed, slump-shouldered and clad only in a pair of plaid boxers, the other Lambda Chis expressed silent thanks that they were not him, even as they longed desperately to be.

But Esquerita was also an accomplished musician and played on recordings with such greats as Jimi Hendrix, Dr. John, Allen Toussaint, and Elvis's backup singers, the Jordanaires. In 1968, he changed his name to the Magnificent Malochi and signed with Brunswick Records, but shortly after that, he began to fade from the music scene, and from here on, Esquerita's whereabouts become increasingly hard to trace. Apparently he spent time in Rikers Island under the name Mark Malochi, and it's said that he performed at African-American gay clubs under the name Fabulash during the 1970s and worked after as a parking lot attendant, still as flamboyant as ever. A few months before his death, he was spotted washing windshields at an intersection in Brooklyn, New York.

Eskew Reeder, Jr. died of AIDS in Harlem on October 23, 1986 and is buried in a pauper's grave.

As a gay, black, flamboyant, gospel-trained and immensely talented singer, songwriter and pianist, Esquerita is the template on which the Architect of Rock 'n' Roll drew his own image. And as an itinerate shape-shifter who changed his name when he had to and flirted with greatness but also crime, poverty and catastrophic disease, Esquerita is the gold standard of what Greil Marcus calls the Old, Weird America. It's hardly surprising that Little Richard mentions him in the White biography; although oddly, considering that he spent enough time with Esquerita to be able to say, as he does in his introduction to Esquerita's 1994 album *Sock It To Me Baby*, "he taught me how to play piano," he doesn't even seem to be sure what his name is.

Sensitive to how much has been stolen from him, Little Richard may find it difficult to admit fully just how much he took from the one entertainer who gave him a model to build his own show on, right down to the Pancake 31 makeup both men wore. The apostle Peter pretended thrice not to know his Savior; Little Richard doesn't go that far, but he might have given more credit to the man who not only saved him from showbiz obscurity but also is more responsible than anyone else for guaranteeing him the worldly equivalent of an eternal afterlife. (In the album intro, Little Richard says that he was actually the one with the pompadour and that Esquerita took the hair style from him.)

But Esquerita provided Little Richard with more

than eye-popping visual imagery. The earliest Little Richard recordings show none of the flair that would make him famous, and even his first New Orleans session for Specialty Records has a generic r 'n' b sound to it — up to a point. And the name of that point is "Tutti Frutti," the full story of which will be told in Chapter 3. But suffice it to say here that, during a break, Little Richard sang and played an X-rated version of The Song That Started It All on the piano of a local café with all the flash and outrageousness that Esquerita would have brought to the task. His producer, who had been worried about the poor quality of the session, not only knew a hit when he heard one but also saw that an over-the-top style would sell the other songs, the ones that had been looking lame up to that point. And the rest is showbiz history.

One more thing about Esquerita is that, by word and deed, he suggested to Little Richard the slipperiness of boundaries: how, for example, it might be advantageous to be a man at one moment and a woman the next. Bands in that day often pretended to be one another; for a while, Richard performed with a group called Melvin Welch and His Orchestra, though Melvin changed his name to Percy because Percy Mayfield and His Orchestra had a hit record that drew the crowds.

Another group in Macon called themselves the Dominions in the hopes that careless fans would mistake them for Billy Ward and the Dominoes, the top r 'n' b group that, for a while, included the Clyde McPhatter whose own name was manipulated for showbiz purposes, since the bandleader often billed him as his non-existent brother, "Clyde Ward."

But nothing says loving like the gender-bending practiced by Esquerita or, even better, the female impersonator Richard remembers only as Bobby, who sold himself to the horndogs at a nearby army base. "Those soldiers would shoot anything down," Little Richard remembers, "bird or bee, tadpole or frog." So polished an artist was Bobby that he left many of his customers in the dark — literally, since some of them didn't even know they'd been with a man. Others got hot and chased Bobby till the high heels broke off his shoes, "but some guys were pleased, you know?"

If you can play in a band that pretends to be another band or look like one sex and be the other, how hard is it going to be to swear off the devil's music and start singing God's or, as Little Richard does today in his stage shows, perform both back to back?

Two other performers are seminal in the shaping of Little Richard's style, and, fittingly, one is a gospel singer and the other a secular showman of the first order. Sister Rosetta Tharpe appeared at the Macon City Auditorium when Little Richard was a child, and he hung around during the equipment set-up and sang one of her songs to her when she walked in. Taken with the little charmer, she called him up on stage that night to sing with her and gave him a handful of money later, though the bigger payoff was the crowd's cheers and applause ("it was the best thing that ever happened to me," he told Charles White).

But even though Sister sang gospel, there's a spirit to her songs that sounds more Saturday night than Sunday morning. And it's not hard to make connections between her music and his. Her version of "Jericho" is based on repeated shouts more than narrative or portraiture, and in that it's a cousin to such Little Richard songs as "Slippin' and Slidin'" or "Keep A-Knockin'." There's no story per se, just one big image ("and the walls come tumblin' down"), as in Little Richard's "I Got It."

Mainly, there's a strong sense of personal involvement, because after enough Joshua-fit-the-battles and well-well-wells to get the blood up, Sister cuts loose with a cry of "I'm goin', goin' 'round the walls of Jericho!" By that time, and whether you're saint or sinner, you want to jump up and dance all the way to the Holy Land.

Along with Esquerita and Sister Rosetta Tharpe, Louis Jordan got under the right guy's skin at the right time. His best-known song, the jump blues single "Caldonia," was, as Little Richard says, the first piece of music he learned that wasn't a church song. "Caldonia" is more sophisticated than anything by Esquerita or Sister Rosetta; it begins with the one-two-three chords of a boogie-woogie piano backed by bass and brushed drums, onto which are added layers of muted and then not so muted horns. Jordan's vocals begin to tell the story of a hard-headed gal who's worth it, though you don't know what her name is.

A minute into it, though, he sets the hook: "Caldonia! Caldonia! What-makes-your-big-head-so-hard?!" After that, that's all you want to hear, all you want to shout along with the vocalist. (Little Richard remembers doing this as a kid.) But if you pay attention to the picture Jordan paints, you'll see that Caldonia is the mother of Long Tall Sally, Miss Molly, Miss Ann, Jenny and especially Lucille, the least cooperative and most desired of Little Richard's musical sweethearts. Like Long Tall Sally, Caldonia is "long, lean and lanky," but the main thing about her is that she's not totally attainable. In other words, she gives a man who's proud of his gal-catchin' skills a chance to show what he can do. And like a lot of Little Richard songs, "Caldonia" refers obliquely to the lure of that fuzzy thing its heroine sits on: the singer's mother keeps telling him not to go over to that gal's house, he says, but "Mama don't know what Caldonia was putting down."

A stage freak, a soul shouter who loves the Lord, a big-band professional driven crazy by a piece of tail: this and much more is Little Richard.

Actually, I wasn't sitting in Willie Ruth Howard's apartment the first time I heard Little Richard's voice. In fact, he welcomed me to Macon — okay, it was a recording, but you, too, can, like me, call the Macon-Bibb County Convention and Visitors Bureau after hours (the number is 478-743-3401) and hear a familiar voice shout "Hi, this is Little Richard, the Architect of Rock 'n' Roll, talking to you from my hometown of Macon, Georgia!"

And then you think, architect? The very word conjures up a larger world, that of Leonardo and Michelangelo, say, who were to Renaissance Florence what Little Richard, Otis Redding and the Allman Brothers were to twentieth-century Macon, the one group making paintings and statues and cathedral domes just as the other made soul music, rock and blues, each in a little, out-of-the-way town and at the same time.

Now how does that work, I asked myself. The Florence answer came easily: the artists there were backed by wealthy merchant families who competed with each other to commission great works. To answer the second half of the riddle, though, I hopped in my car one warm day in August and headed to Macon itself. Why not? After all, Little Richard had invited me.

Located on the banks of the Ocmulgee River, Macon is a town of 97,255 citizens at last count. It's also a virtual anthology of nineteenth- and early twentieth-century architecture, from Federal and Victorian styles through Art Deco. It seems that General Sherman had Macon on his check list during his infamous march to the sea, which began with the burning of Atlanta and left a 60-mile-wide path of destruction before ending in Savannah, but left the town untorched when he had to move his troops quickly to fend off an unanticipated Confederate attack. Notable among the buildings are the many Greek Revival homes on Cotton Street, one of which now houses the 1842 Inn, where I spent my first nights there.

That doesn't mean that Macon is unchanging; in my time there, it opens into view and disappears and then, just when you're about ready to get back into your car and head off to Augusta or Savannah, it pops back up, somehow different from what it was before.

Maybe this is because my first trip to Macon was

in the steamy depths of August. To make sure I got a proper entree into the town, I'd gotten a commission from the *Washington Post* to write a travel article; this took me to places the ordinary gawker doesn't get to go. Understandably, much of my piece was on the Macon music scene, then and now. I focused on three clubs that, of the many in town, seemed to be premier venues: Jazz Plex, 550 Blues and the Hummingbird Stage and Taproom.

But when I came back to Macon six months later, all three clubs had closed. One, the Hummingbird, had just reopened, and there was talk that 550 Blues would be up and running soon. Jazz Plex had an ominous-looking chain and lock on the door, and people didn't seem to want to talk about it. That's the Macon I know: here, gone, back, coming back soon, never coming back.

When Macon's on, though, it's really on. Centered on a genuine walk-around downtown instead of sprawled out over busy thoroughfares that lead to strip malls and suburbs swollen with tacky McMansions, Macon is Your Other Home Town; no matter who you are, it'll fit you well.

It's also a town where you can see just about every human type in the course of a 5-minute stroll. During intermission at the Grand Opera House, old-timers from the Carlyle Place retirement community knock back shots of Wild Turkey and look around with that expectation of amusement that people have when everything has turned out better for them than they ever thought it would. A couple of blocks over, an outdoor tableful of brokers from Fickling & Company celebrate a huge commercial sale over sizzling fajita platters at a Mexican restaurant called Acapulco. On Cherry Street, lookalike twenty-somethings with glossy hair and pipestem legs dart from club to storefront club, scanning the regulars for their friends before darting off again like gazelles across a concrete veldt.

Yet Macon is also where I've had some of the weirdest conversations in my life; part of its hometown feel is that you get the idea that you might have lived there years ago, although you're not quite sure where the "there" was or even who you were then.

One night a guy who looks like a caveman in a faded red tee shirt introduces himself with a grin as Salty Dog and tells me he's a promoter based in Scottsdale, Arizona who travels the states setting up car auctions. I ask him how that works, and he gives me a 5-minute short course on car auctions, though a minute later, he confesses that he's actually a high-end house painter who never has to advertise because he's the best in the business, and he lives here in Macon but works mainly in the well-heeled Buckhead area of Atlanta, though none of this matters, really, because what he really is is a musician. . . .

Behind him, a heavily tattooed man in a sleeveless tee with a baseball hat and a helmet-strap beard shouts, "You must have enjoyed your time in jail, because you're going back there!," though he's not shouting this at anyone I can see.

A minute later, a bald guy with a huge zirconium stud in his ear says he wants to "solicitate" my opinion on something, but I suspect the conversation will result in a cash transaction from which I will not profit; I'd already given up $88 that day to Little Richard's cousin Willie Ruth, and I didn't know how many more hits my travel budget could take. So I keep walking till I find a spot on a bench — Macon is a bench-rich town, which makes ambling in it especially pleasurable. Before long, I'm joined by one of those men who, though unhealthily skinny in the chest and limbs, look as though they've had a basketball implanted between the muscle sheath of the abdomen and the outer layer of skin. "The way I see it," he says, "you can take somebody from here," at which point he makes the "here" gesture, "and take them to there," and now he's making the "there" gesture, "and bring him back," and his hands flit from "there" to "here" again as he winds up his proposition by saying, "and he won't be the same person."

Now observations on that level of profundity call for a response, and my new friend's cocked brow telegraphs that he's expecting one from me. For a moment, I'm stymied, so I decide to play it safe: "Well . . . reality is reality," I say. "See!" he says as though I've just explained the Special Theory of Relativity. "That's what I'm saying!" And I say, "All right, then," even as I'm wondering what the fuck we just said to each other.

All of this is to say that Macon is a handmade world still. Sure, it has streetlights and running water and stuff, but there's a real sense of improvisation, of a town being put together before your eyes. Sherman's men may be fiddling with their matches, but they're a few miles to the east and don't even suspect that Macon's there; nothing's ever taken away from Macon, so everything's still right where you can find it when you need it, whether you need it or not.

Ray Davies of the Kinks once said he was liberated as a songwriter when he listened to a live recording of John Lee Hooker's "Tupelo, Mississippi" and heard a car horn in the background, realizing then that songs had imperfections in them because they were made by imperfect people — like himself, say. In Macon, you can hear the car horn, and it wakens you to a new life, one you used to know.

One thing Macon has plenty of is stories. Everybody has at least one, and Southern politeness prompts them to share: again and again, someone would warn me that so-and-so's stories were to be taken with a grain of salt, but that didn't stop them from urging me to hunt that person down and squeeze that unreliable narrative out of them.

Actually, provided I could get someone to hold still long enough, I didn't have to do any squeezing at all. One thing I learned about pulling out a notepad and introducing yourself as a journalist is that one out of ten persons will drop what's in their hand and head out the door, because they're up to something they don't want you and the readers of the *Washington Post* to know about. The other nine, though, will say something along the lines of "See, back in 1993 ..." or "Now I ain' know him, but my momma do," and you're off.

At the Convention and Visitors Bureau, there's a video in which locals speculate as to why so much great music came out of such a tiny town. And no fewer than three of these thinkers offered that "there must be something in the water."

Fine. It was broiling outside, and I intended to drink my fair share of water during my stay. First, though, I needed something solid after four hours on the road, so I stopped in at the Market City Café, where I had the warm meatloaf sandwich with homemade chips and coleslaw. The owner said his meatloaf recipe was his grandmother's, which naturally meant that the particulars couldn't be divulged, though he did insist that I try Market City Café's signature banana pudding, which came in a fried flour tortilla bowl that had been dusted with cinnamon and sugar.

It was so delicious that I raved about it to everyone I met during my three-day stay in Macon, which turned out to be a little like claiming that the baby you just saw is more beautiful than all the other babies in town. "I'll put my banana pudding up against theirs any time" was a typical response, as was "No, baby, you got to try my mama's before you can say you had real banana pudding." Hmm. Could it be that the wellspring of local musical talent lay not in the water, after all, but in a creamy dessert?

There was only one way to find out, but first I figured I'd confront the music head on, so I walked over to the Georgia Music Hall of Fame, just two blocks away. The exhibits are organized as "villages," each devoted to a different genre: jazz and swing, gospel, rhythm and blues, country, and so on; there's also a kid's area that features such hands-on displays as a drum kit and a composition station where you can press buttons, see notes appear on an overhead screen and then hear your opus played back.

The list of annual inductees gives a sense of the extraordinary range of music found in a single state: there's Johnny Mercer, who wrote "That Old Black Magic" and "Moon River," but also James Brown, Lena Horne, Chet Atkins, groups like R.E.M. and the B-52s, Capricorn Records founder Phil Walden, and soprano Jessye Norman. Recognizing the importance of collaboration in the music business, the Hall of Fame makes a point of inducting both entertainers and background players, so the first induction ceremony, which took place in 1979, honored Ray Charles but also music publisher Bill Lowery.

Little Richard was inducted in 1984, and his online citation encases him predictably in the acrylic of scholarship. Much like the Jehovah of Deism, who is thought to have set the world to ticking like a great fat clock and then retired to the sidelines, this Little Richard is described as a Prime Mover who isn't Moving very much these days: "although he was only a hitmaker for a couple of years or so," says the citation, "his influence upon both the soul and British Invasion stars of the 1960s was vast, and his early hits remain core classics of the rock repertoire."

In Macon itself, though, Little Richard is as alive as ever. Walk into the Tic Toc Room, where the singer got his start, and customers will show you where the stage was where he sang, even though the stage isn't there any more; meanwhile, the bartender is scrambling for photos of the old days, ones which show the young Richard in shirt and tie instead of the outrageous robes he favors these days, though his head is back, his mouth is open, and it looks as though he's about to fly to pieces.

It was at the bar of the Tic Toc that I met Tommy Barnes, a young health care administrator, who told me his parents had gone to school with Little Richard and knew he was going to be an entertainer even then because, when the teacher left the room, the precociously outrageous Mr. Penniman would put the trash can on her desk, sit on it, and sing "Sitting on the slop pot, waiting for my bowels to move," which, as Tommy sang it, sounded uncannily like Little Richard's 1956 hit "Slippin' and Slidin'."

Much of what Tommy told me jibed with Willie Ruth Howard's tales of the young Richard's exuberance, how he beat out rhythms on every surface he could find, sang Louis Jordan songs, and followed a musical vegetable vendor around the neighborhood as he sang about his wares. The result, of course, was "I Got It," the song about "the little old man with the billy-goat cart," ostensibly a paean to black-eyed peas, butter beans and collard greens, though buried among all that produce are lines that express the quintessential Richardian truth, namely, "It ain't what you do, it's the way how you do it / It ain't what you eat, it's the way how you chew it."

Of course, Willie Ruth is not one to address the sexual

allusions in the lyrics of her celebrated cousin. A godly lady, she's also not one to risk scandal by entertaining a gentleman unchaperoned, so the day I spoke with her, her grandson Vincent Harrison sat in on the interview. As I asked her questions, frequently she would answer "I don't know!" and then, when Vincent offered a response, jump in to embellish and say whether she agreed or not.

But when I asked her what was the one thing that made Little Richard a star, she gave me her most decisive answer of the day, saying instantly "The family!" and then going on to speak especially of his mother's reciprocated love ("When we were playing, he'd say, 'I got to go check on Momma' and run away and come right back. At four years old!"). You don't have to have a degree in psychology to know that the unconditional love of a mother is the one thing that can give someone the courage to . . . well, to be Little Richard.

It was Vincent who, while Willie Ruth stepped out of the room at one point, told me that he saw a vital connection between Little Richard and Macon, for Jesus, too, had come from a small town, "a place called Nazareth, which means 'unrevealed.' The good things always come out of the unrevealed."

I checked on the etymology later, and it's likely that Nazareth took its name from a Hebrew word for "sprout" or "shoot." But, hey — in both cases, the truth was unrevealed, and then it sprouted forth. And the world hasn't been the same since. Shakespeare came from Stratford, Leonardo from Vinci, Michelangelo from Caprese (near Arezzo, itself a small town), James Brown from Augusta,

Otis Redding and Little Richard from Macon. All other things being equal, a hungry youngster from nowhere will make his mark.

Another day in Macon, I spent the morning riding around in the truck of Little Richard's friend Seaborn Jones, who used to work for the *Mr. Rogers* TV show and then as a veterinarian's assistant, though he has chronic pain issues now after being attacked by a skunk. Seaborn's a good poet as well; he's got some nice publications to his credit, and he's the author of such works as "Why Talk to Strangers? There's Nobody Stranger Than Me."

Seaborn is also white and sounds a little like Deputy Dawg when he talks, though he's a bit more aimless than the canine sleuth. At one point he drawls, "David, ah'm afraid there's not going to be any car chase in this conversation." Actually, there's a car chase in every conversation with Seaborn; he drew for me a one-of-a-kind portrait of Little Richard, one I'll share in Chapter 5.

That same day, I spent three hours with Alan Walden, Phil Walden's brother and manager of Otis Redding and Lynyrd Skynyrd. Still handsome and impish, Walden can't resist acting out his tales of life with Otis and Little Richard and the Allman Brothers. Over lunch, as he tells me how Skynyrd lead singer Ronnie Van Zant almost beat a "skanky-ass groupie" to death in a motel room, he sticks a butter knife in my face and threatens me so convincingly that the other diners in the restaurant we're in look alarmed, and for a moment, I myself hope they're thinking of piling on Alan the way the band eventually jumped Ronnie and quelled his murderous instinct.

A Georgia Music Hall of Fame inductee himself, Alan knows everybody in the business, and he led me to a dozen other great Macon storytellers whose tales are in this book.

My only knock against Macon is that it wears me out every time; when I get back to my bed, I have to stay in it like a kid who's been sent to his room because he's had too much sugar. Locals will say I'm romanticizing it, but to me, Macon is a magical town. When I'm there, I'm never sure whether it's 2009 or 1909. And when I leave, I always wonder if Macon will be there when I come back.

Yet it'd be wrong to pretend that Macon didn't suffer from the same problems other Southern cities did, notably the acid bath of racial injustice. As I type these words, I'm looking at a photo on my desk I took of beautiful Macon Terminal Station, a magnificent building built in the Beaux Art style in 1916 and Georgia's grandest surviving railroad station; in 2002, it was purchased by the city of Macon and converted to a retail center. Over the northern archway, you can clearly see the words "Colored Waiting Room" carved into the building's stone surface. Maconites I talked to said it was decided to leave the entryway unchanged as a reminder of a time when an entire race was treated as though they were animals.

That wasn't so long ago, but it was long enough that, to anyone born after 1960, it can seem like something that happened on another planet. My white students play and study with and date black students and vice versa, and to them, the idea of the one race grinding its boot into the face of the other is inconceivable. I envy them their innocence.

Because the truth is such that any sentient being would want to look away. Most visitors to Macon have paused before the historic Douglass Theatre. Here pioneering DJ Hamp Swain, who featured a young Little Richard in his band the Hamptones and later was among the first to put James Brown on the radio, held the weekly *Teenage Party* and talent contest that Otis Redding won so many times that finally he was banned from the show. Yet surely none of them know that, a few years before Little Richard's birth, one of the ugliest incidents in the town's history took place there.

On July 29, 1922, a young black man named John "Cocky" Glover shot up a pool hall, mortally wounding two patrons and killing outright a deputy who had come on the scene. Glover eluded arrest for two full days but finally was taken off an Atlanta-bound train and returned to Macon, where he was seized by a mob of white men and killed with shotgun fire. His body was then paraded through the town's streets and eventually dumped in the foyer of the Douglass Theatre; somebody called for gasoline, but police arrived before the body could be incinerated. One of the witnesses to the violence was a laborer named Elijah Poole, who left with his wife and two children as soon as he could and moved to Detroit, where he changed his name to Elijah Muhammed, eventually becoming the leader of the Black Muslims; later he would write that he had seen "enough of the white man's brutality in Georgia to last me for 26,000 years."

But white violence in the region was far from over. Little Richard was two years old when Claude Neal was tortured and killed just over the state line in Marianna, Florida. Neal, who had been accused of killing a white woman, was scolded, castrated and hanged; some accounts have him being forced to eat his own genitals.

The biggest case of racial violence, of course, was the killing of Emmett Till for the crime of flirting with a white woman. Till was beaten and his eye gouged out before he was shot in the head and thrown into the Tallahatchie River with a weight around his neck; the outrage that resulted was one of the seminal events that resulted in the organized civil rights movement that changed America forever. Sound like ancient history? Emmett Till was murdered in August of 1955, less than three weeks before Little Richard recorded "Tutti Frutti."

Of course, the average black person didn't suffer anything approaching the violence visited on men like Glover, Neal and Till. But the threat of that violence was part of the air they breathed, and it poisoned their lives. Like young Elijah Poole, a Mercer University professor named G. McLeod Bryan finally couldn't take it any more and left Macon in 1956, saying later, "When I left Georgia I left because I said there's no way you can breathe in Georgia. You can't go get a hamburger, you can't go to the drugstore, you can't take a bus ride, you can't go to a ballgame, you can't go to church, can't go anywhere, without race. And I said that's stifling. Who wants to spend your life in a place in which every single moment of your existence had to do with race?"

When you walk down Cherry Street in Macon these days and see blacks and whites working and relaxing together, the nightmare of the middle of last century seems almost unbelievable. I asked Alan Walden why white hatred was so heated then, and Alan replied, "Well, those were just uneducated people, David." Then he paused for a second and shot me that choirboy grin of his before continuing, "Or, as Phil and I used to call them, stupid motherfuckers." I asked Alan if he and Otis Redding had ever hung out, and Alan said he drove with Otis to a drive-in once for Cokes and hamburgers, but Otis was visibly fearful and slumped down farther and farther in the passenger seat until he disappeared from view.

Little Richard met the racial challenge, though he did it musically, not politically, by integrating the dance floor. In Ken Burns's *Jazz* series on PBS, narrator Keith David calls jazz "an improvisational art making itself up as it goes along — just like the country that gave it birth," and so is rock 'n' roll. In the same series, Wynton Marsalis comes on screen to say that "if you were a slave, you had to learn to improvise."

Little Richard was no slave in the legal sense, but his formative years were spent in a world where whites could cheat, steal from and even kill blacks with impunity. Melville's Ishmael, little more than a slave himself, said, "A whale-ship was my Yale College and my Harvard," and Little Richard, too, learned more than he knew from a hellish world he couldn't have escaped anyway.

After one trip to Macon, I find myself home again in the middle of the night. I'm too tired to look over the notebook I've filled during my latest foray, so I heat up some leftover fried chicken I've brought back with me and put on an episode of the TV series *Friday Night Lights* I've been meaning to watch.

Like a lot of my Netflix choices, I picked this one because of a write-up in the *New York Times* that praises the show for its novelistic bigness. While derived from Buzz Bissinger's wonderful account of small-town life, the *Times* writer says repeatedly, this television show is not just about football.

Everyone who has never been to the South, and especially Northern journalists, are experts on that part of the country. Trained reporters who wouldn't dare venture an opinion on Iraq or Pakistan because they've never worked in those countries are happy to tell you about life in Dothan or Bainbridge, because, well, everybody knows what those people are like down there. Actually, *Friday Night Lights* is about nothing but football, and it takes the sport as a metaphor for Southern boobishness in general. Its treatment is cliché: the quarterback is cleancut and true to his girl, and when he's hit hard and paralyzed, the backup QB bumbles his way through a star-is-born debut. The coach is a sad-eyed idealist, and his wife is a materialistic shrew who loves her man but not as much as she loves her dream house with its his-and-hers closets. The black players are loud, stupid and Christian, the whites rednecks or drunks, the girls virgins or tramps. None of them ever takes an algebra test or conjugates a verb in any language other than English.

ˉOlder men in the town are rich and willing to pay any price for a victory. Their wives are slutty dipsos; they belong to book clubs, but they ask linemen if they'd like to "blitz" an older woman. Grandmas are senile, grandpas dead. Nobody is fat. Everybody is mushmouthed, and no one is very bright. No one in the whole show has a sense of humor, which will be news to anybody who has spent more than 5 minutes this side of the Mason–Dixon line.

Mainly, there are no surprises. In reality, the South — the real South, not the McSouth of popular imagination — is one big surprise. On the last day of my first visit to Macon, just when I thought nothing could catch me unaware, the local newspaper's front page disclosed that Mayor Jack Ellis had sent a declaration of solidarity to Venezuelan President Hugo Chavez, a vocal ally of Iran and Cuba and a leader who has called President Bush "the devil."

High-level disagreements notwithstanding, said Ellis, what's wrong with supporting someone who's in favor of subsidizing the cost of heating fuel for low-income citizens? Judging from reactions on Cherry Street, half the paper's readers were upset about the prospect of socialism while the others were wondering, "Where's Venezuela?" Chavez himself, no doubt, was asking, "¿Donde está Macon?"

On the one hand, I don't mean to romanticize the place. On the other, I can't wait to get back there. For one thing, I've got a lot more banana pudding to eat.

I don't love Macon the way Little Richard does, but I understand why he loves it so much. All in all, Macon took a goofy little boy named Ricardo Wayne Penniman and changed him into a grown-ass man, into the love-maker/heartbreaker/soulshaker the world knows as Little Richard.

CHAPTER 2

The Ninety-Nine Names of the Prophet

There was black, there was white, and then there was black and white. There was jazz and rock and hip-hop, and then there was — what? All along, there was pandemonium, fevered mingling, one tribe swapping their pretty beads and shiny mirrors for the pelts and dried fish of another, and for that we should be grateful. Or at least resigned, because American culture has one great theme, race, and one great art form, pop music, and the two are and will always be inseparable, will always be the twin helices of our national DNA.

I was born in the last days of World War II, when the phrase "civil rights" wouldn't have meant much to anybody, at least not in Baton Rouge, Louisiana. The races mixed freely, but only up to a point, and entirely unself-consciously. Everybody knew where to go, what to do, and how to do it, and this knowledge was so thoroughly ingrained that it was another 20 years before any of us even thought about going somewhere our great-grandparents hadn't been and doing something new and doing it in a way that hadn't been done as far back in one's family as one could remember.

The day began with the arrival of Dot, my "black mama," and Alphonse, the Haitian yardman. My mother was a schoolteacher and my father a college professor, but we lived on a working farm, so my brother and I were feeding chickens or watering horses as Dot began cooking and cleaning and Alphonse sharpened his tools. The schools we attended were segregated, but at the end of the day and on weekends we played with black children, such as Siebel and David, whose parents worked on the much larger Burden plantation down the road.

Siebel was close to my age, and often he and I listened to the radio and danced, if you call yelling, throwing our arms in the air, and rubbing our fannies together dancing. Moving from the all-white world of school to a mixed one before and after was effortless; I certainly didn't question it, and nobody else seemed to notice, either.

Each different kind of music had its place, too. My parents favored classical music, but, in what I'm sure was an effort to hook my brother and me on "good" music, they tended to choose works of a syrupy or bombastic nature: *Scheherazade*, *Bolero*, the toreador song from *Carmen*, *Peter and the Wolf*, the "William Tell Overture." We listened dutifully, even making up our own lyrics to songs we couldn't understand, though when the older folks weren't around, my brother, who was four years older than I was, would put on the jazz discs he had somehow managed to slip into the house.

His need for secrecy didn't have a racial basis; by that time, the idea that black music was subversive had come and gone. Fats Waller may have raised a few eyebrows, but Gershwin made jazz respectable, which meant that, if white bands played it and it was okay to listen to them, then it must be okay to listen to black bands as well; besides, Benny Goodman's band was mixed-race, and it played at Carnegie Hall. Still, who wants to listen to his parents' music? If you're a kid and you're not trying to define yourself through music that your parents would find different, possibly incomprehensible, and maybe even repulsive, you're not doing your job.

But if my parents had caught my brother and me listening to Art Blakey and the Jazz Messengers and found all that riffing outrageous, they hadn't heard anything yet.

It's 1955, and America is sturdy, white and asexual. The country basks in post-war prosperity, and Dwight and Mamie are in the White House. True, Alfred Kinsey has just published his reports on male and female sexual behavior, but — well, Dwight and Mamie are in the White House. Besides, Kinsey's big news is that most sex happens when people are by themselves. Ninety-two percent of males he interviewed reported having masturbated. Can you believe it?

Meanwhile, as slightly more than nine of the ten men on your block are wiping their hands on a washrag and explaining to their wives that they're too tired to have sex tonight, a gay black cripple from a town nobody every heard of is about to record a hymn of praise to the joys of heinie poking.

And millions of Americans are turning on their radios to hear, not Mitch Miller's spunky march through "The Yellow Rose of Texas" or Andy Williams's hyperglycemic version of "Autumn Leaves" or some other forgettable single from the 1955 hit parade but a jungle cry that may or may not have been "A-wop-bop-a-loo-mop, a-lop-bam-boom!" No chords served as warning; no hup-two-three horn section or soothing violins announced that a song was underway, just this savage scream. And there was more to come: "Tutti frutti!" shouted some crazy guy, and then "Aw, rootey!" or "rutti" or even "Rudy." Who the hell is Rudy? And isn't "tutti frutti" a kind of ice cream? The music charged ahead, too fast for most people to follow, and from time to time that nut would scream out that "A-wop-bop!" noise again. What the hell's going on here? What the hell does any of this mean? And if you can't understand it, what's he hiding? Could it be that guy's shouting about . . . *sex*?

You betcha. Actually, all of Little Richard's best songs are about sex: "Long Tall Sally" treats Uncle John's adultery with the temptress of the title, for example. But nothing's as juicy and loosey as the song that was about good booty until it all got cleaned up, as we'll see in Chapter 3.

A couple of years later (on December 11, 1957, to be exact), ABC television aired an episode of the long-running series *The Adventures of Ozzie and Harriet* called "Tutti Frutti Ice Cream" in which the patriarch of America's ideal (read: hopelessly square) family goes in search of the eponymous foodstuff, though when some-one asks him what tutti frutti is, Ozzie's reply is "Well, it's kind of hard to explain." I'll say. But then life in America has never been easy to explain.

Okay, it has and it hasn't. Sure, there's an official explanation for America: Columbus landed in 1492, the Pilgrims came along a few years later, the cowboys tamed the West, people drank a lot of cocktails during the Jazz Age, we kicked Hitler's butt, hippies smoked a lot of pot and then became baby boomers. But there's a little more to it than that, and to understand the culture that Little Richard comes from and represents better than anyone else, we could do worse than to begin with our country's very name. "Strange," Ralph Waldo Emerson wrote, "that broad America must wear the name of a thief. Amerigo Vespucci, the pickle-dealer at Seville, who . . . managed in this lying world to supplant Columbus and baptize half the earth with his own dishonest name."

So while it'd take more space than is available to write America's unofficial history, one can make a start, begin-ning with the fact that the man who gave his name to this country was, as the first line of the best book about him says, a pimp and a magus. Hero and villain, salesman and sorcerer, Amerigo Vespucci was, according to Felipe Fernández-Armesto's *Amerigo: The Man Who Gave His Name to America*, possessed of "quicksilver tongue, feath-erlight fingers, infectious self-confidence." The term "pimp" might be a little harsh; the author himself backs down at one point and says "procurer" might be more accurate, since Amerigo acted as a go-between for certain friends who had amorous interests. But as a Renaissance Florentine, he certainly practiced sorcery — what great man of the time did not?

So how did a poser get an entire continent named for him? After all, Columbus both beat him to the land mass and was the first to identify it as a new continent. But effective public relations work will always trump fact. Convinced by accounts of Vespucci's voyages that were later discovered to be fabrications (not by Vespucci but by his followers), in 1507 cartographer Martin Waldseemüller produced a map on which he gave the new continent a Latinized version of Vespucci's given name. Waldseemüller came to doubt Amerigo, and in a subsequent map labeled the new continent Terra Incognita instead. It was too late, though. The "Vespucci industry" had triumphed: there's no greater force in human affairs than effective branding.

But even a successful ad campaign will fizzle if there's nothing behind it. It took a couple of centuries to get things going, but the America we know today was built from scratch by a motley gang of jackleg entrepreneurs with little interest in the continent's indigenous peoples and every desire to pursue what would later be called, without a shred of irony, "life, liberty, and the pursuit of happiness."

Here is Richard Kluger's capsule summary of America's early settlers (from his *Seeking Destiny: How America*

Grew From Sea to Shining Sea): "Crafting their own destiny with whatever tools were at hand, they gained a continental expanse by means of daring, cunning, bullying, bluff and bluster, treachery, robbery, quick talk, double-talk, noble principles, stubborn resolve, low-down expediency, cash on the barrelhead, and, when deemed necessary, spilled blood." And every time new territory became available, it was immediately invaded by soldiers, squatters, peddlers, and other intruders of every kind, scofflaws and scapegraces whose descendants walk the halls of our statehouses and corporate suites today.

Those descendants may preen and pretend that, when they sit on the toilet, vanilla ice cream comes out instead of the usual stuff, but while they have long since brushed the last speck of red Georgia clay from their Bally loafers, the truth is that they are the sons and daughters of a rough-and-tumble America that's as real as the chrome-and-glass one. It's the same America Little Richard comes from, only he's not afraid to admit it.

And he should know. When Willie Ruth Howard was shuttling in and out of the room with the purse I'd put $88 in, her grandson Vincent told me not to feel different from anyone else and to recognize that Little Richard will always have a chip on his shoulder, especially where money's concerned. Later, I'd understand what he meant as I watched a conversation between Little Richard, Chuck Berry and Bo Diddley that's part of the Taylor Hackford documentary *Chuck Berry: Hail! Hail! Rock 'n' Roll!* (1987). The talk went this way:

BO DIDDLEY: Money. . . . You know, I set up all night, looking at the contract, trying to figure out how I was going to make any money out of two . . . two. . . .

CHUCK BERRY: Half a cent a record.

LITTLE RICHARD: Well, you had to sell two records to make a penny.

CHUCK BERRY: Now a record cost 59 cents; that means 58 cents were going somewhere else.

LITTLE RICHARD: Now I, I, I . . . whoo, boy!

CHUCK BERRY: I majored in math. I was looking at the other 58 cents.

LITTLE RICHARD: I majored in mouth! I was doing all the talking and no walking. I couldn't even understand the contract. When I got it, all I wanted to see was "Little Richard." When I saw that, I thought, "Whoo — I've got a contract!"

The situation was actually worse than this conversation suggests. If you do the arithmetic yourself — and this will be the only time I ever correct Chuck Berry on anything — you'll see that, when he and Bo and Richard made a penny, someone else was making $1.17.

But the exploitation of early rock musicians (largely black) by producers (largely white) is well documented and needn't be repeated here. Suffice it to say that these latter-day shysters and con men are the true sons of the bilko artists who preceded them — that, in a manner of speaking, they came by their calling honestly.

The country I'm describing, the one that sports a slouch hat and a toothpick and has a Case knife in one pocket and a rigged contract in the other, is a country Greil Marcus calls the Old, Weird America, a land of itinerants and con men and riverboat gamblers, a place described in the poems of Whitman and the songs of Bob Dylan, an America that once was and still is, if you know where to look. The Old, Weird America is "a kind of public secret," says Marcus, "a declaration of what sort of wishes and fears lie behind any public act."

In his book-length description of this invisible empire, Marcus offers no better introduction to the Old, Weird America than Harry Smith's *Anthology of American Folk Music*, a 1952 Folkways Records issue that is now available as a set of six CDs. Comprised of everything from country blues to Cajun social music to Appalachian murder ballads originally recorded between 1927 and 1935, the anthology set Dylan and a thousand others like him on a road of discovery. In Marcus's words, it was Dylan's "first true map of a republic that was still a hunch to him." And as Little Richard was born in 1933 in a town as handmade today as it was then, these songs map out the world he came from.

Not the world he created, of course: there are some up-tempo songs here, but nothing anyone would call rock 'n' roll. Yet Marcus sounds as though he's talking about "Tutti Frutti" when he says a typical song here "may be a sermon delivered by the singer's subconscious, his or her second mind. It may be a heretic's way of saying what could never be said out loud, a mask over a boiling face."

Little Richard's most famous song is a cleaned-up version of a paean in praise of anal intercourse; does that not sound like "a heretic's way of saying what could never be said out loud"? With "Tutti Frutti," as with the songs Harry Smith collected, it's as though you're looking at a painting of official America, of a town square with a church and a bank and a courthouse past which men stroll in shirts and ties and women push baby carriages. Then, pow! There's a tearing sound, and Little Richard's pomaded head bursts through the canvas, his mouth wide in song. "For the first time," writes Marcus, "people from isolated, scorned, forgotten, disdained communities and cultures had the chance to speak to each other and to the nation at large. A great uproar of voices that were at once old and new was heard, as happens only occasionally in democratic cultures," though when it does happen, it's always "with a sense of explosion, of energies contained for generations bursting out all at once," like the nonsense syllables Little Richard roars at the start of his iconic song.

I've called the Old, Weird America a handmade world, and it's true; it's not a world of monumental figures posing like statues in a park or at least not only that kind of world. The times I'm writing about in this book are the times of Fats Domino, Little Richard and Chuck Berry, but also Jesse Belvin, Thurston Harris and Ed Townsend.

Big name groups like the Platters, the Drifters and the Coasters would dominate the charts, but there were also the Turks, the Pharoahs, the Flairs and the Penguins. There were big-name DJs like Casey Kasem, Alan Freed and Murray "the K" Kaufman, but also such small-timers as Bugs Scruggs, Okey-Dokey, and Georgie Woods, "The Guy With the Goods," all of whom played their part on a stage that shook with sound and fury.

The Old, Weird America is everywhere, and it's always been invisible. It's not as though mountebanks and card-sharps and banjo players strolled down the thoroughfare in broad daylight; the sheriff would just catch up with them that much sooner, and besides, their clientele preferred the shadows. Just as the burghers of Boston and Philadelphia never saw the Old, Weird America 150 years ago as they made their way from banks and law offices to their townhouses and back again, we don't see it now if we choose not to.

And one more thing about the Old, Weird America: it's not all fun. I don't let my students get nostalgic over the Sixties that they never knew; there was sex and acid and the Jefferson Airplane, yeah, but also sit-ins and lynchings and head-whippings, not to mention that war we lost in Southeast Asia. So taking a swig from my own bottle of patent medicine, I don't let myself get sentimental about Walt Whitman's America. We laugh at the King and the Duke in *The Adventures of Huckleberry Finn*, but Pap is a drunk who beats the son who eventually stumbles across his father's drowned and bloated body.

Slavery is real in that work of fiction, just as it was in

America for 300 years. Funny thing is, it's real today: a woman I know who directs a refuge for battered women says that every time we pass through a crowded Wal-Mart, we walk by people who work for no money, who've been smuggled into this country and are too traumatized and afraid of their handlers or the law or us to pull on our sleeves and ask for help.

Even when we're looking the truth right square in the face, we don't always see it. We can see the present-day Little Richard in concert or catch his 50-year-old shows on YouTube. But how different his career is when we reflect that he recorded his biggest hits just weeks after Emmett Till was murdered. And by 1964, when James Chaney, Andrew Goodman and Michael Schwerner were killed in Neshoba County, Mississippi, Richard had long since called a halt to a career that would revive only fitfully. His are some of the greatest songs in the rock canon, yet their birth is bracketed by the ugliest murders of the Civil Rights era.

And those murders might not beat in your blood, but they're real to plenty still. So much of what we do as human beings results in outcomes that are at least different and often the opposite of what we intend, yet lynching has exactly the effect its perpetrators intend. *New York Times* columnist Bob Herbert quotes a Willie Banks who remembers seeing photos of Emmett Till's disfigured face, with one eye shot out and a bullet through the skull (Till's mother insisted that the world see what the killers had done to her son). "Those pictures really stuck in my mind," he says. "And the message I got was that if I stepped out of my place, that could happen to me. You shouldn't have to think that way, but that's the way I thought." Willie Banks was 12 years old when he saw the photos he still sees today at the age of 66.

Out of all this pain comes music that tells us that we, too, are alone, though the music takes it one step further and says that we're not helpless, either. Life hurts like a motherfucker; music heals at something approaching the same rate of speed.

Little Richard's Macon was a small town in his childhood — it's not that big these days — but it was big enough to attract the traveling shows that offered their gumbo of hokum and glitz and freakiness and showmanship. The shysters and sideshow acts and hoodoo men gave little Richard Penniman the exact list of ingredients he'd need for his future showbiz career, just as they showed him how to mix everything together in a way calculated to conjure a quarter out of a sucker's pocket.

And Macon itself produced not a few of these hucksters, including the proprietor of Dr. Hudson's Medicine Show, which the hyperactive youngster joined the way another kid would climb aboard a slow-moving freight train without having any idea where that act might take him. "I didn't tell anybody I was going," he tells Charles White; "I just went." Doc sold a patent medicine that was supposed to cure everything: rheumatism, arthritis, leg trouble, toe trouble, whatever ailed you.

Medicines of this kind have always been a part of rural Americana. The cure-all when I was a kid was named for

Dr. George Humphrey Tichenor, a physician who was a longtime Baton Rouge resident and was said to be the first Confederate doctor to have used antiseptic surgery in the performance of battlefield surgery. From there he branched out to other ailments, even other species. Dr. Tichenor's Patent Medicine consisted of just three ingredients — alcohol, oil of peppermint, and arnica — and each bottle came with a small-print label on the back that told the owner how to use it to address a wide variety of complaints of both man and animal.

Probably even closer to Doc Hudson's juice was a product called Hadacol, developed not by a physician but a four-term Louisiana state senator with, in the tradition of Phineas T. Barnum, the ideal huckster's name of Dudley J. LeBlanc. Marketed as a vitamin supplement, Hadacol, too, contained a fair amount of alcohol, which was listed on the label as a "preservative" and enhanced its appeal to, among others, an aunt of mine whose Christian views didn't allow her to drink, though she did take her shot of Leblanc's elixir four times a day, as directed. Leblanc sponsored the last of the big-time medical shows, the Hadacol Caravan, which featured Hank Williams, among others. And the medicine gave its name to such appropriately named tunes as "Hadacol Bounce," "Hadacol (That's All)," "Drinkin' Hadacol," and the best known of them, "Hadacol Boogie," recorded most recently by Jerry Lee Lewis on his 2006 *Last Man Standing* album. As long as there's music, there'll always be an Old, Weird America.

Doc Hudson operated on a smaller scale, but he used

the same formula: for marketing, I mean, not medicine. Music and a road map and the promise of a panacea: this is Old, Weird Americana at its best. And considering that he had to cover the same territory more than once (like a traveling piano player), he had to deliver the same quality product consistently (like a traveling piano player). And while the stuff in his bottle can't have fixed everything it promised to cure, there must have been something that kept audiences coming back as surely as a music-loving audience will keep buying concert tickets and records from an entertainer who keeps delivering.

In an audience where virtually no one had an office job and everybody lifted, toted and hauled for a living, bodily pain was pandemic. No doubt Doc Hudson's "snake oil" had a hefty alcohol component, like Tichenor's Antiseptic (as it came to be known) and Hadacol, so that whether you rubbed it on or swigged it or both, it had some effect. Too, it cost less than a trip to a real doctor, for one thing, and for another, you got to see a show for the price of your bottle. It was as part of Dr. Hudson's Medicine Show that Little Richard sang "Caldonia" while somebody else played the piano. And when you see his live shows today, see him come out in his spangly suit and stir up the audience and interrupt his piano banging to hawk $20 posters, you can see the ghost of Doc Hudson hovering in the wings, shaking his head at his disciple's shenanigans.

Then there was Macon's so-called town prophet, Dr. Mobilio, a showman whose outrageous demeanor may have been even closer to the future entertainer's eventual aspirations. Because whereas Doc Hudson sold snake oil, Dr. Mobilio sold something even better — he sold hope. "He was a spiritualist," Little Richard recollects, who sang to draw a crowd to which the doctor would prophesy. A descendant of the Sibyl of Cumae, who wrote prophesies on oak leaves and then scattered them to the winds, Dr. Mobilio tinkered with the process, letting people write questions on pieces of paper which he destroyed. His was a kind of reverse prophecy in that he then told the people what their questions were, though his answers had a Cumaen vagueness to them that allowed listeners to make of the prophet's words what they would. "Boy, you're going to be famous," Little Richard recalls him saying, "but you're gonna have to go where the grass is greener!" Sage advice for an ambitious boy whose world was pretty much limited to the city limits of Macon, Georgia.

What Dr. Mobilio contributed to the entertainer's eventual stage persona was twofold, because he showed the young Richard Penniman that people wanted something to believe in, something bigger than a cure for muscle aches — something like religion, in other words, whether you called it that or not. And he also showed him how to sell that product, which is that you sell yourself first.

This isn't new advice. Berry Gordy, Jr. of Motown Records said he learned everything about business from his mother, who ran an insurance and real estate business and told him that if you sell yourself to people first, they'll like you and will buy whatever you're offering.

Since Dr. Mobilio wasn't hawking whole life policies or corner lots, he tailored his self-presentation to his unique market niche. He wore a turban and a red and yellow cape, Little Richard remembers, and the boy would sing to attract customers; within a few years, Richard would put two and two together and become both the singer *and* the flamboyant dresser. *And* the showman hawking his wares: you hear the true voice of small-town huckstering in the blown Royal Crown Hairdressing commercial on the Specialty Sessions (disc three, cut eight) when Little Richard tries to convey his enthusiasm for the grooming product to DJ Gene Nobles but repeatedly calls him "Gene Noble" and a "disc jerky."

Leaving nothing to chance, Dr. Mobilio also had a particular talisman that people turned out to see and that he called the Devil's Child, which was "the dried-up body of a baby with claw feet like a bird and horns on its head." Had enough of organized religion, be it Bud Penniman's Seventh Day Adventism or some other variety? Or maybe you just need to supplement your traditional beliefs with something from the other side, the way folks would go see their regular doctor if they had a fever they couldn't quite shake but take a slug of Doc Hudson's snake oil if they just wanted to treat a bad back.

Either way, like Doc Hudson, Dr. Mobilio knew the importance of signs and symbols, of icons — of branding, to use a term that would never have occurred to either of them. It's no surprise that, like these backwoods healers with their limited repertory, Little Richard sings the same songs over and over, pausing during his performances to shout their names over and over again, like a litany: "'Jenny . . . Jenny . . . Jenny,'" he says at the end of "Jenny, Jenny" on the live *Little Richard's Greatest Hits* album, dragging out the spaces between each word, and then, in a rush so fast you have to listen repeatedly to hear how many song titles he's fitting in, "LongTallSallyTutti FruttiRipItUpReadyTeddyTheGirlCan'tHelpItShe'sGot It!" Where the variety comes in during his shows is in the songs he covers by other artists as well as his where'd-that-come-from stage patter, but his songs don't vary.

Why? Because they work, like a good bottle of snake oil. At the end of "Good Golly, Miss Molly" on the *Greatest Hits* album, you can hear the entertainer take on the powers of the healer as he starts out in a quasi-religious way, saying, "Wherever you are, I've been there. Wherever you've gone, I've gone. I'm back." But then he says something that shocks even a non-religious person. "I want to let you know that I Am That I Am," he cries, which is blasphemy: according to Exodus, it's what God answers when Moses asks to know His name. Then, without so much as a breath, Little Richard calls out to someone, "Come on, Grandma, get your chair and come up and listen," and, paraphrasing Jesus when he called forth the sick, says, "My music is the healin' music. . . . It makes the blind see, the lame walk, and the dumb and the deaf hear and talk!"

Often, the more rigid a cultural characteristic, the greater the likelihood of its opposite being just as strong, if less apparent. So while it's well known that these United

States were shamefully (because legally) divided along racial lines in Little Richard's youth, what's just as true but less discussed is that there was often racial mingling of the most fruitful kind.

The best recent book on country music, Dana Jennings's *Sing Me Back Home*, addresses the exchange between classic country and rhythm 'n' blues that enriched both. Folks who listen to Johnny Cash like Fats Domino, too. Ray Charles's 1962 album, *Modern Sounds in Country and Western Music*, is credited with helping to move country into the mainstream, but three of its songs ("I Can't Stop Loving You", "Born to Lose" and "You Don't Know Me") were also top ten hits on the rhythm 'n' blues chart. Chuck Berry's "Johnny B. Goode" not only sounds country but takes as its subject a country boy, the lyrics say, who never learned to read or write so well though he could play a guitar like ringing a bell. In concert these days, Little Richard regularly covers "I'm So Lonesome I Could Cry," "Jambalaya" and other Hank Williams classics; his cousin Willie Ruth Howard told me "I'm So Lonesome I Could Cry" is his best live song and her favorite.

Georgia Music Hall of Fame curator Joseph Johnson told me there was constant exchange between country and r 'n' b musicians in the early days and that one of Little Richard's favorite groups was Uncle Ned and the Hayloft Jamboree. Johnson put me in touch with Pee Wee Clark, who played steel guitar for Uncle Ned and now makes his home in Brisbane, Australia; Clark was inducted into the Australian Country Music "Hands Of Fame" in 1980. In 1953, he and the band became part of broadcasting history when they made the transition from WMAZ radio to television and become one of the most popular programs on WMAZ-TV, where they did a noon or afternoon program every day for an hour and a night-time program once a week.

In an e-mail to me about Little Richard, Clark writes: "I knew him . . . as an entertainer when he was at the Tic Toc restaurant [sic] on Broadway in Macon. We only had the casual meetings, mostly on the road coming from our different places of work, mostly in the early hours of the morning. We talked about the business and how we were doing. I know he had a great respect for Uncle Ned and all of us in the Hayloft Jamboree Gang. We were on WMAZ-TV at the time. He always had a good word for us," writes Clark, and then, commenting on the racism that was a barrier to the success of Little Richard and other black musicians, "if things were not the way they were back then, I'm sure he would have been invited to appear on our show! But . . . things were as they were, and that's that!"

Little Richard's position on the Macon social scale was further complicated by talk about a liaison that seems unlikely, in retrospect, though any relationship between a flamboyant performer and a lady nightclub owner whom some might have thought too big for her britches would have generated gossip. Clark writes: "I do know there was a big stink about him and 'Ann,' the lady that owned the Tic Toc. Many people were talking about he and she being . . . how shall I put it . . . 'too close.'"

Opened in 1951, Ann's Tick-Tock Club was a rare

venue in that it was one of the first truly integrated gathering places of any kind in Macon. This may have something to do with that great leveler of humanity, the military. There were numerous bases nearby, and when our fighting men hopped out of those uniforms and escaped from their by-the-book routine, it stands to reason that at least some of them were going to head for a place where all were welcome regardless of race or sexual orientation. And if there was a joint in town where gender-bending and race-mixing were allowed and maybe even encouraged, the Tick-Tock was it. Little Richard even used the name of Ann Howard, the owner, in his song "Miss Ann."

The Tick-Tock closed as a nightclub in 1975 and the building deteriorated for about a quarter century. In 2000 the building was purchased by a Connecticut restaurateur and gutted; an upscale restaurant called the Tic Toc Room now occupies the space where a more rough-and-ready venue once stood. "There was the usual talk of drugs and all that garbage," continues Pee Wee Clark. "I was never in the place during this time, so can't say for sure, but I do know there were drugs around, and some musicians were into them." Little Richard was one of these: "They shoulda called me Little Cocaine, I was sniffing so much of the stuff!" says the singer in *The Life and Times of Little Richard.* My nose got big enough to back a diesel truck in, unload it, and drive it right out again." (Setting the record straight, Pee Wee Clark says, "My favorite drugs back then was a Winston cigarette and a cold beer! Don't do the cigs anymore, but love a cold beer!")

There are plenty of black versions of country songs out there, such as the ones on the *Dirty Laundry* CD, which includes James Brown's jaw-dropping version of "Your Cheating Heart." And listening to any half dozen mainstream country songs from the Fifties and then an equal number of r 'n' b tunes is enough to convince any listener how the two genres speak to each other. Throw in a graphic or two — for example, a photo of Bill Haley and the Comets, big-shouldered smirking Caucasians who look as though they could pump out either country or r 'n' b at the whim of the flat-top cats and dungaree dolls in the audience — and the case for the one influencing the other is made.

After all, country music describes so many of the snares and pitfalls that r 'n' b does. Classic country has one subject, prison. This means prison-prison, yeah, but also the jailhouse of drink, poverty, violence, ill health and faithlessness ("Being cheated on is a living death borne in the midst of everyone who knows you," Dana Jennings writes). Not doing time at the moment? Country music says you will.

And it has a single lighting scheme: none. Most of the old songs sound as though they were thought up "on starless nights on snake-black roads," according to Jennings. Many are set in or near coal mines. Black jeans and a pearl-buttoned black shirt were the Saturday night get-up of many a rockabilly Rigoletto (Tom Waits's phrase for Roy Orbison) before they became the official uniform of Johnny Cash, the Man in Black.

Black looks, black hearts, black circles around your

eyes when you've been up all night with a sick child who's not getting better or because you lipped off to some squirt who turned out to be meaner and quicker than you are: black is the color that dominates the country palette. Not to mention the blackness in the eyes themselves: in a photograph of a father he barely recognizes, Jennings sees in his stare "a country darkness . . . that scares the hell out of me."

And then there's the blackness of skin color. One of the secrets of the Old, Weird America, the one of medicine shows and bootleggers and itinerant bluesmen trying to stay one step ahead of the sheriff, is that blacks and whites mingled there, not in schools or courthouses or other public institutions but on a porch where people got together to sing or, if somebody had the money, around a Sylvania record player to whose tonearm someone had taped a nickel so it wouldn't skip. Carl Perkins's 1956 hit "Blue Suede Shoes" was a #1 country song, but it was #2 on the rhythm and blues chart. A year later, the Coasters and Sam Cooke had songs in the r 'n' b top five, but so did Elvis and the Everly Brothers. Out of this amalgam of country and r 'n' b came the mightiest musical force of our day: Dana Jennings writes that "Blacks and poor whites always had more in common than either cared to admit — just ask the men and women who accidentally created rock 'n' roll."

In another well-written and authoritative study of roots music, Mark Kemp quotes a Crystal Lunsford as saying this:

How come you think music's so good in the South? It's because black people and white people worked together to make it so damn good, that's how come. There's always been black people in white southern music and white people in black southern music. That's the way it works down here. We wouldn't have a southern rock & roll without the black influence, but then, I don't think the blues and rock & roll would have been as accepted if it weren't for white people down here who backed them and pushed them and recorded them. It took both races. Music has always been a universal thing down here. It goes beyond color. And that goes all the way back to slavery.

By the way, Crystal Lunsford isn't a professor or a music critic. As Kemp explains, she's a third-generation employee of the Eveready plant in Asheboro, North Carolina who lives by herself in a trailer in rural Guilford County. If you're the kind of expert who doesn't look beyond the obvious, you might think the musical world is as segregated as the school systems were back in the day. But if you live out in the woods and you keep your eyes and ears open the way Crystal Lunsford does, then you know there's more to the picture.

When director John Sayles was researching the background of his film *Honeydripper*, which tells the story of a rural Alabama tavern owner in 1950, he says, "I found a book that had some playlists from jukeboxes in Mississippi back then, and the interesting thing . . . is how different and eclectic it was." According to Sayles, "There was blues and gospel and country-western that was pretty close to rockabilly already. There was swing music still. There was that Louis Jordan small-combo jump music. There was rhythm and blues, and there was Bing Crosby. And then there was this proto-rock 'n' roll stuff, all on the same jukebox. The country guys were listening to blues, and the blues guys were listening to country."

To the pioneer performers, then, the most influential music of our times was as black and white as the 88 keys on a piano. After that, though, what happened? Music critic Sasha Frere-Jones analyzes the re-segregation of American music in an essay where he juxtaposes two concerts by the Canadian band Arcade Fire, a name which, judging from how often my students mention it, is about as popular as a band can get these days. The first concert, writes Frere-Jones, was "ragged but full of brio," and he recalls spending the evening happily pressed against the stage. But by the second concert, the band's limitations couldn't be hidden any longer: "I was weary after six songs," he writes, because "if there is a trace of soul, blues, reggae, or funk in Arcade Fire, it must be philosophical; it certainly isn't audible." What was missing was "a bit of swing, some empty space, and palpable bass frequencies — in other words, attributes of African-American popular music." (Frere-Jones's views set off a firestorm of debate; among the more measured responses is that by Carl Wilson in *Slate*.)

After all, rock 'n' roll is "the most miscegenated popular music ever to have existed." Why, then, did rock undergo a "racial re-sorting in the nineteen-nineties"? The time when black and white kids danced to the same music was brief and it was tense, but it existed. Besides, in racial terms, all times are tense: the race issue of the day centers on Hispanic immigration and its myriad nuances involving drivers licenses, health care, bilingualism and so on. But that's just today, and it's just Hispanic: can the Chinese be far behind?

I wrote earlier about my black playmates Siebel and David, boys I raced with, fought with, laughed with, climbed trees and built forts with, danced with. They dropped off my radar at some point, but years after I had left Baton Rouge to begin my adult life, I came back once to visit my parents and read in the *Morning Advocate* that Siebel had been shot to death by his step-daughter; he'd had too much to drink and begun hitting family members with an iron chair, and then the bullet stopped him.

By this time, I was a tenured professor with a wife, a child of my own, two cars, a mortgage. The professor in his corduroy, the dead man on the kitchen floor: you can't imagine two more different endings. But for the longest time, it seems, we were the best of friends.

In the midst of the many savvy things Dana Jennings says about country music, he makes a larger point about our shifting culture. It wasn't the Sixties that unhinged America from an Ozzie and Harriet world view that never existed in the first place. The change came long before that, from a "blighted world of physical hunger, hope, and pleading" that was forged by the Great Depression and World War II and out of which came fatalism but also selfishness, two emotions that needed to be integrated in some kind of way.

Up stepped r 'n' b and country: "after World War II, during which both men and women had tasted unparalleled freedoms amid a shadow that at times had felt like the end of the world, it was going to be hard to keep couples happily down on the farm." Pop music persisted in the fantasy that all was right with the world, while jazz, as redefined by bebop, "retreated into insider virtuosity." If Americans wanted music that told them they were standing on shaky ground, they had to turn to the earthy sounds of country and r 'n' b.

And they did. And the music more than met them halfway, because it told the truth about life, which is that it ends someday, so we better start ricking up our hair and scrounging in the sofa cushions for gas money. Pop treats death as an inconvenient rumor, and the d-word is not even in the jazz dictionary. Rock 'n' roll was a few years away, and its appeal lies in the fact that it tells us we're going to live forever.

But rhythm 'n' blues and country understands that "there's music to be found in the sound of dirt cascading onto a coffin," writes Jennings, "and art that's willing to grapple with death is art that lasts." If the music changed, that's because the world changed first. Dorsey Dixon wrote "Wreck on the Highway" in 1936, says his son, Dorsey, Jr., "when the '36 Fords came out with a V-8 engine and began to kill people all over the nation." More power, more uncertainty; more uncertainty, more art.

No wonder there's a fierce ambivalence to the best country music. On the surface, Johnny Cash's "I Walk the Line" is an ode to fidelity, but he wrote it for his first wife, Vivian Liberto, whom he left for drugs and touring and, eventually, June Carter. "I keep a close watch on this heart of mine," the song begins, but as Dana Jennings says, you only keep a close watch on something you can't trust.

Hank Williams's "Hey, Good Lookin'" sounds pretty innocent, but when it came out in 1951, after the war and the Holocaust and Hiroshima, who was innocent any more? The singer says he's going to throw his date book over the fence, but what big-boned gal in her right mind doesn't believe he'll notice exactly where it lands?

The same is true about almost every Little Richard song. "Tutti Frutti," we know, is about something other than ice cream. "Good Golly, Miss Molly" is about a gal who "sho' likes to ball," but I don't think he's talking about dancing. Somebody's slippin' and slidin' in "Slippin' and Slidin'," but in what? "The Girl Can't Help It," meaning she can't help what? "I Got It," at long last, but what's the it that I got? And all along, the Miss Ann of "Miss Ann" is "doing something no one can," and I'm betting that that something has more to do with the carnal realm than with cookery, say, or fine needlework.

The words often say one thing, the music another. In the realm of sacred musicians, the divide's even more obvious. Many a gospel lung-buster has walked out of the revival tent and found himself in the backseat of a

Ford with a hottie and a pint of busthead whiskey while his amps were still smoking. But sometimes it takes wild men and women to break art's stale paradigms: John Berryman, Sylvia Plath and Anne Sexton made shambles of their lives but also injected poetry with a vitality that's still there, just as the Sex Pistols diverted mainstream rock into a new channel, at least until its bass player stabbed his girlfriend to death and killed himself with a heroin overdose. Sick kicks and hot licks: sometimes they go together. Or, as Dana Jennings reminds his readers, Jerry Lee Lewis wasn't kicked out of Southwestern Bible Institute in Waxahachie, Texas for splitting hairs over Christian doctrine.

We're all lonely, then, we're all scared, and mainly of the Grendels we share a cave with. But, and this is the point of country music, we're somebody. The best country songs are like the best of anything: they tell you you're tough, even though the whole world is against you. Hell, you're tough *because* the whole world is against you. All that meanness made you what you are, made you into "Jimmy Brown, the Newsboy," the shoeless but proud hero of the 1951 Flatt and Scruggs song who says "don't look at me and frown" to the businessmen who buy his papers. He's a polite kid, but something in his voice tells you that you'd rather sandpaper a bobcat's butt in a phone booth than go toe to toe with that pint-sized entrepreneur.

Every song in the classic country pantheon is there because it tells you you are somebody. Webb Pierce's "There Stands the Glass" makes you glad you aren't an alcoholic, because you love the stuff so much you'd never want to give it up. George Jones's "He Stopped Loving Her Today" makes you, too, want to love someone so hard that you won't quit till your breath leaves the circle of your teeth, just as it makes you long for such a love. If you can listen to Merle Haggard singing "Mama Tried" and not miss your own mother, it's because she's sitting there with you and probably missing hers. Patsy Cline's "I Fall to Pieces" reminds me that I haven't — yet.

Is this not just as true of every song in the rock pantheon as well, even if the song you're listening to isn't about you in a direct way? Take Little Richard's songs about women: cue up "Long Tall Sally," "Jenny Jenny" and "Lucille," and instantly either you are those women or the one who loves them or both. Move the needle to "Rip It Up," and suddenly it's Saturday night and you just got paid, even though, in reality, it's Monday morning and you're flat broke. Now try "Heebie Jeebies." See what I mean? You have the heebie jeebies now! You're somebody with the damned heebie jeebies, and you're proud to be that person!

Nobody ever says that, of course. But in rock's secret meanings lies its power. In another Greil Marcus book, *Lipstick Traces: A Secret History of the Twentieth Century*, our most astute cultural critic says that when Malcolm McLaren, who would later manage the Sex Pistols, heard a fellow student sing "Great Balls of Fire" in a grammar school talent show, he recalls that "I'd never heard anything like it — I thought his head was going to come off."

And here's how Pete Townsend of the Who characterizes the power of rock:

> Mother has just fallen down the stairs, dad's lost all his money at the dog track, the baby's got TB. In comes the kid with his transistor radio, grooving to Chuck Berry. He doesn't give a shit about mom falling down the stairs . . .. It's a good thing you've got a machine, a radio that puts out rock and roll songs and it makes you groove through the day. That's the game, of course: when you are listening to a rock and roll song the way you listen to "Jumpin' Jack Flash," or something similar, that's the way you should really spend your whole life.

No wonder the grownup world worried about real African Americans like Little Richard and faux ones like Elvis. If, as Marcus says, real life meant "the pleasurable consumption of material goods within a system of male supremacy and corporate hegemony," the kids wanted something else entirely — or thought they did, which was good enough to get rock 'n' roll out of a few scattered clubs and into every American living room. And beyond: the rise of rock was paralleled by the spread of the transistor radio, which came along in November 1954 when the Regency TR-1 was marketed for $49.95 or nearly $400 in today's dollars. That's a lot of cabbage for Sis and Junior, but before less expensive models came along, about 150,000 TR-1s were sold, meaning at least that many kids were willing to pony up that much to get away from the square sounds dripping out of Mom and Dad's squat console. With the new handheld units, the music could go anywhere.

And there's one more thing about primal rock 'n' roll, that is, rock before it became the industry it is today. The first rock will always be the best rock because it was itself, which was huge, yeah, but it was also more than itself. All pop music functions as entertainment and also a mirror of its listeners' fears and passions: I listen, therefore I am. But Richard Meltzer, one of the earliest rock critics, says the first rock came at a time when the world was changing, and it wasn't long after Little Richard's pioneer efforts delivered a new attitude toward race that the music as a whole functioned as a delivery system for an entire spectrum of new behavior: drug use, sexual freedom, new attitudes toward women and minorities, a new kind of politics. "Without the music, drugs would have delivered nothing, the Vietnam protests would have delivered nothing. Music was the cutting edge of everything," says Meltzer. And, boy, did it cut: "it was like the beast that controlled everything was losing its grip."

What do the kids want? They don't know: any pop musician can say, as blues singer Johnny Shines did, "The public don't know they want it, but they know there's something that they want from me. Otherwise they wouldn't be climbing onto me. . . . I know it's the next thing. I got the thing that they want. They just don't know what it is."

One of the most powerful lyrics in rock history comes

in the first verse of Smiley Lewis's "One Night of Sin," where the repentant vocalist confesses that "The things I did and I saw / Would make the earth stand still." What are those things? A 14-year-old kid wouldn't know, but from an adult perspective, it sounds as though the singer was involved in a scene of Old Testament pagan proportions: an orgy, maybe, or at least painful and violent sex fueled by booze or uppers or just the take-no-prisoners savagery of the id. Now a teen wouldn't say any of that, but he might say the song makes him think of something like freedom. No wonder, in Elvis's version, where "one night with you" is substituted for "one night of sin," the evening in question is what the singer is "praying" rather than "paying" for, and the joyful horror of the first verse is wiped away when he sings that "The things that we two could plan / Would make my dreams come true." In the episode of the *Bill and Ted's Excellent Adventures* cartoon where Mozart time-travels to Macon to play twin pianos and sing "Good Golly, Miss Molly" with Little Richard, the two musicians censor themselves and substitute "we sho' had a ball" for the forthright "sho' likes to ball" of the original.

Not that you can really blame anyone for disguising the sexy, race-mixing nature of rock 'n' roll. Little Richard's heyday was what Russell Sullivan calls the Age of Simplicity. "There was no room for dissidence" during the Fifties, he writes; "it simply wasn't tolerated. Everyone was expected to embrace the prevailing vision, beliefs, values, and modes of behavior." The figure Sullivan calls Fifties Man was "a family man, loyal, respectful of authority, patriotic, religious, innocent, pure, hard-working, decent, modest, friendly, gentle, likable, simple." Maybe three of those adjectives apply to Little Richard, if that. Yet he and his studio knew it and went to extremes to court, not the kids, but their parents. The liner notes to Richard's second Specialty LP say that "in selecting the songs for this new album, Little Richard tried to top his first album . . . [and] included some unreleased material for his fans' parents who still may not 'dig the beat.' He feels that if they'll only listen to songs they remember like 'Baby Face' and 'By the Light of the Silvery Moon' done up in the Little Richard style, they'll enjoy this new album, too!"

At its best, rock's too big, too magical, too scary to go unsupervised. When the sloppy garage-band anthem "Louie Louie" broke into the top ten in 1963, the song was banned on many radio stations because of the supposed profanity of lyrics which graphically depicted sex, according to the kids who, like me and my friends, "translated" the band's mumblings and passed them from desk to desk in study hall. The FBI even became involved, though the agency's 31-month study concluded with a report that investigators were "unable to interpret any of the wording in the record."

In *Lipstick Traces*, Greil Marcus says that when the first all-girl punk band the Slits say "Fuck you," they're really saying "Why not?" So what is Little Richard saying when he shouts "A-wop-bop-a-loo-mop, a-lop-bam-boom!"? The same thing the Slits are saying when they shout "Fuck you!"

In the Seventies, of course, four white girls from London could say what couldn't be said in the Fifties by a gay black cripple in Georgia. According to what the Macon Meistersinger told Charles White, when his dishwashing job got too hot and heavy, he'd cuss out his boss in nonsense syllables. When the traffic in pots and pans became too much, he'd shout, "A-wop-bop-a-loo-mop, a-lop-bam-boom, take 'em out!'"

In other words, why not?

CHAPTER 3

Keep A-Knockin'

As both James Brown and Smokey Robinson point out, Little Richard began with piano-driven rock; his boogie-woogie piano recalls the use to which that instrument was put in the big-band music of the 1940s. To this melodic structure he adds the infectious beat of funk, defined by music historian Anne Danielsen as "bass-driven, percussive, polyrhythmic black dance music, with minimal melody and maximum syncopation." What a combination: to the vast musical potential of the piano is added the funk that, as Danielsen says, is "a difficult thing to play properly, because it should in fact be played everything *but* properly." Indeed, the song that changed the music forever is a most improper song.

Let's look at the next stage of the journey its creator traveled in order to reach that spectacular level of impropriety.

In his essay "Fate," Ralph Waldo Emerson writes that

"in different hours a man represents each of several of his ancestors, as if there were seven or eight of us rolled up in each man's skin — seven or eight ancestors, at least; and they constitute the variety of notes for that new piece of music which his life is."

Dr. Nobilio, Dr. Hudson, Esquerita, Sister Rosetta Tharpe, Louis Jordan, Brother Joe May, Billy Wright: as Richard Penniman searched for the self he would be, these and a dozen others, including, no doubt, ones he himself has forgotten the names of, marked paths that led to roads that led to highways that led back to paths again, and somewhere at the heart of this maze stood a performer whose name was Little Richard, though nobody knew that yet.

The trip wasn't easy. In Charles White's biography, Richard recalls hanging around a club in Fitzgerald, Georgia but sleeping in a field at night and eating hand-outs of offal ("chitterlings and pigfeet and all the stuff I won't even eat today"). It was there, though, that he was taken up — kind of — by a band called B. Brown and His Orchestra. Brown and the other musicians didn't like him very much, Richard recalls, but he could sing better than they could, so he started performing with them.

The band traveled through Georgia and Florida, eventually making its way to Macon. Peggie, the performer's sister, recalls that the band's station wagon had a placard taped to it with "Little Richard" on it, that being the first time anyone in the family had heard the name. Even Papa Penniman relented — a little. "Daddy hadn't wanted him to go on the road to sing. But when he saw that he couldn't hold him back, he sort of accepted it and didn't say too much." As a preacher and under-the-counter businessman himself, Bud knew you had to walk the walk as well as talk the talk, so he even backed off on the pompadour issue: "When Richard left he didn't have one because Daddy didn't want him to and he was very strict. But now Dad felt that it was part of the makeup of an artist, so he wasn't annoyed."

B. Brown and His Orchestra gave Richard's showbiz aspirations a shove forward, but there was too much shovin' and tusslin' behind the scenes, and before long the hyperkinetic performer was jumping from one group to another like a Georgia bullfrog: Sugarfoot Sam from Alabam, the King Brothers Circus, the Tidy Jolly Steppers, the L. J. Heath Show, and the Broadway Follies, whose home was Bailey's 81 Theater on Decatur Street in Atlanta. If the word "circus" looks out of place in this list, it shouldn't: Richard uses words like "carnival" and "minstrel show" when he recalls his days with performers who pretty much did what they wanted — that is, what their audiences wanted — in a day before the mainstreaming of an act's image made entertainment into an industry and prices started going up so that men in suits could make money off freaks and geeks. Gospel, comedy, belly dancers, sideshow oddities, cross-dressers (including you know who): for a while there, the Old, Weird America was on stage, and everybody could afford a ticket.

Little Richard was a man of his time, and while he enjoyed the adulation ("I thought I was famous then"), he was ready for brighter lights. It was in Atlanta that he met Billy Wright, he of the clothin' and shoethin' the apprentice performer admired, and it was Wright who got him into the recording studio for the first time.

Now performing is one thing. The crowd is there to have a good time, and virtually every member of it has helped him or herself to enough caffeine, alcohol, dope, or all three to insure that the ride is a long and riotous one. Crowd enthusiasm is infectious, and the infection can be spread through the gimmicks and high jinks of which Little Richard would one day be the undisputed master. Bette Midler has spoken ruefully of her overreliance on sheer natural endowment when things started going bad in the house: if the audience was snoozing, all she had to do was lock her thumbs in her tube top and, in her words, "go for the tits." On stage, Little Richard never leaves anything to chance. He always goes for the tits.

But recording is a much crueler mistress: you might please an audience eventually, but before you do that, you have to please one cold-hearted son of a bitch, your producer. If you're lucky, that SOB is going to be the best in the business; that is, somebody who has heard hundreds of singers sing thousands of songs and knows a hit when he hears one. This is a guy who doesn't smile much, somebody sipping coffee and wearing a drip-dry shirt and skinny tie while the band members sport hepcat outfits and sip, smoke, or snort something stronger. If you're lucky, your producer is someone who has yanked off his headset and stomped out the studio door on those days when your body's there but your mind and your voice are someplace else and who won't quit until he has wrung the best out of you.

Little Richard first steps into a recording studio in Atlanta in 1951, when he is 18. He tries to imitate his idol, Billy Wright, but he lacks Wright's dynamics, possibly because this is the first time he has sung without a live audience to give him the yells, whistles and waves that drive his show forward. He produces one hit that sells well in Atlanta and Macon, a song called "Every Hour," but in an occurrence that became commonplace in his career, the song is re-recorded by Billy Wright himself as "Ev'ry Evenin'" and eclipses Little Richard's version.

In 1952, Little Richard cuts four new tracks, but these, too, go nowhere. It's also the year that his father, Bud Penniman, who has finally come around to his son's music and even proudly plays "Every Hour" at his club, the Tip In Inn, is shot to death by an unruly customer.

In 1953, again Little Richard cuts four tracks; not only do these tank as well, but in a clash over the singer's swagger and attitude, he is beaten by Peacock Records owner Don Robey and suffers a hernia that won't be repaired for years. In a later session, he cuts four new tracks for Peacock, but these are never even released.

Little Richard keeps a-knockin' on the door of showbiz success, however, and in 1955 sends Specialty Records a tape in a wrapper that producer Bumps Blackwell describes as "looking as though someone had eaten off of it." The songs on the tape show promise, but probably Little Richard would never have recorded again had he not hounded the staffers at Specialty till they agreed to bring him into the studio for a final try.

This time, all that persistence pays off.

Born Arthur Goldberg in 1917 in Greensburg, Pennsylvania, Art Rupe listened to the singing that came from a local black Baptist church and came independently to the conclusion that others were arriving at in the post-war years: that the future lay in "race records" which, as Rupe saw it, featured "a big-band sound expressed in a churchy way."

The Jewish producer heard something in Christian song that he wasn't hearing anywhere else. "Gospel was my favorite type of music," Rupe says in Peter Guralnick's biography of Sam Cooke, whose early group, the Soul Stirrers, he recorded, "not for religious reasons but because of the feeling and the soul and the honesty of it. To me it was pure, it wasn't adulterated, and that's why I reacted to it."

But Rupe was no romantic: when he arrived in LA with $600, he invested $200 in a stack of black vinyl 78s that he listened to till they turned gray, he says. Armed with a metronome and a stopwatch, he studied the length and beat of each record but also its lyrical content as well as its overall feel. "Some of the music moved me so much it brought tears to my eyes," he recalls, but he also says "I established a set of rules or principles which I felt would enable me to make commercial records."

Rupe started Specialty Records in Los Angeles in 1946; there he recorded Percy Mayfield, Louis Jordan, and other performers from Little Richard's youth, and it was in LA that he hired legendary producer Bumps Blackwell. In 1952, Rupe traveled to New Orleans because he was drawn to the sound of Fats Domino; it was on this trip that he discovered and then recorded Lloyd Price.

Rupe's biggest New Orleans coup was to come three years later, but the trip starts in LA. By this time, Specialty was moving from gospel into rhythm 'n' blues, and Bumps Blackwell had a strong intuitive feel for Rupe's belief in the primacy of feeling in the music, that an imperfect song which took the listener on a real roller coaster ride would sell much better than a technically adept record that stayed in a safer emotional range. Since imperfection's pretty hard to quantify, this meant taking risks, looking in odd places, missing at least as often as connecting, and flying by the seat of one's pants in a way that no classic jazz or big-band producer would even consider.

It also meant opening a package that looked like something the cat had dragged in. In the late winter of 1954 or early spring of 1955, Blackwell recalls in the Charles White biography, Rupe had told him to find a singer to compete with the R. C. Robinson who had changed his name to Ray Charles, stopped imitating Nat "King" Cole and signed with Atlantic Records, where his unique voice would make millions for everybody. So one day this nasty-looking reel shows up; Blackwell plays the tape and hears a poor quality version of two gospel-sounding pieces, "He's My Star" and "Wonderin'." Yet Blackwell was convinced the singer's voice, which was churchy and bluesy at the same time, had . . . something.

Art Rupe wasn't so sure. He did his best to keep the singer at a distance for seven or eight months, but in cases like this, Little Richard is the one who decides how wide or narrow that gap's going to be. Every fourth or fifth day, Rupe remembered, Little Richard called from Fort Lauderdale, Jacksonville, Atlanta: wherever the road took him.

Rupe maintains he never would have signed the singer if he hadn't been so aggressive, but he and Little Richard did have one thing in common, which was a love of the music of Fats Domino. Wondering if lightning might not strike twice, then, Rupe decided to record Richard in New Orleans, at the same J & M Studios where he had recorded Lloyd Price. The fit might have been even better than Rupe himself knew, because it was Price himself who had driven to Macon in his black and gold Cadillac and told Little Richard to send an audition tape to Specialty in Los Angeles.

Down in the Bayou State, a record shop owner named Cosimo Matassa had a recording studio that grew, as did others at this period in the industry, out of his jukebox business. Since the jukes tell you which records people like, why not make the records yourself and make money at both ends?

This didn't mean you had to put a lot of money into your facility; remember, we're going for feeling here, not technical precision. According to the 30-page book that comes with the three-disc *Little Richard: The Specialty Sessions* box set, the room built onto the back of J & M

Amusement Service on North Rampart Street in the city's French Quarter was all of 16 by 18 feet in area; the control room was about the size of four phone booths, and the mixing board itself was no bigger than a small suitcase. It had four knobs, one for each mike and a knob to adjust the overall track level; as Matassa struggled to find a balance in the control room, the musicians moved about the tiny studio, looking for the best mike positions for solos and also for the arrangement as a whole. Earlier I said that Little Richard came out of a handmade world, and you can't get much more handmade than Cosimo Matassa's little shoebox of a recording studio.

Out of this little room with its three mikes streamed the music of the future. From 1945 to 1956, J & M Recording Studio rolled out major hits by black artists, terrifying parents, turning preachers' faces purple with rage, and sending kids to the dance floor. In February 1954 alone, four of the top ten hits in the Billboard charts came out of a room that was almost an afterthought, a rough addition to a record store that was itself barely that (Matassa sold refrigerators and waffle irons, too) on the corner of Rampart and Dumaine.

J & M's first hit was "Good Rocking Tonight," a party song recorded by gospel shouter Roy Brown long before Elvis made it famous. Then musician, bandleader, composer and arranger Dave Bartholomew brought in the Fats Domino with whom he co-wrote many hits that attracted the attention of Art Rupe in LA. Ray Charles both recorded and produced songs there, and a 16-year-old from Ferriday, Louisiana named Jerry Lee Lewis saved his money and traveled to J & M to make his first recording years before he found fame at Sun Records.

All that with "three mikes and some juggling," as Cosimo Matassa tells interviewer Todd Mouton. "If you talk to Dave Bartholomew, he'd tell you that it was 'O.J.T.,' on-the-job training. We learned as we went. New Orleans was not exactly a pillar of technology. There wasn't any place I could go to somebody else's studio and learn something." But if Cosimo wasn't dwarfed by towering banks of computer-controlled sound technology like today's engineers, that was okay, he says: "it forced me to learn how to do it well."

A decade before Berry Gordy, Jr.'s Detroit megalith that became known as Hitsville USA started beaming black music into the bedrooms of white teenagers, J & M Recording Studio was the Old, Weird America's Motown.

Now the musicians Matassa worked with were the best in the business. Essentially, they were Fats Domino's session men, which means not only were they skilled in their individual craft and used to working well together but also that they had nailed that sax-based New Orleans rhythm 'n' blues sound that had savvy producers all over the nation cocking at least one ear toward the Crescent City. Little Richard had already recorded a half dozen of Domino's songs and mastered the Fat Man's "rolling" piano style, so it looked like a perfect fit between singer and band.

Except that it wasn't. As Bumps Blackwell says, the first

few takes were okay, but it wasn't what he was looking for. They recorded some Penniman originals, such as "Lonesome and Blue" and "Wonderin'" and "All Night Long"; they also covered the classic "Kansas City" by the great songwriting team of Jerry Leiber and Mike Stoller as well as "I'm Just a Lonely Guy" by a local named Dorothy La Bostrie who was always pestering Blackwell to record her music. "I had heard that Richard's stage act was really wild," the producer told Charles White, "but in the studio that day he was very inhibited. Possibly his ego was pushing him to show his spiritual side or something, but it certainly wasn't coming together like I had expected and hoped."

One of my Macon interviews was with Hamp Swain, the DJ who, more than any other, was responsible for breaking the race barrier in the Fifties and making sure the world knew about Otis Redding, James Brown and other Georgia music greats. But before that, Hamp had a band called the Hamptones, and Little Richard was the lead vocalist. I asked Hamp if Richard was timid when he performed with his band. "Not exactly," he said. "It was a matter of being around people he knew, whom he could feel comfortable with. Yeah, he could be a little shy around strangers. But when he was with our band, he could be himself." That's it in a nutshell: in New Orleans, Little Richard was cut off from the family and friends that constituted his support system. Worse, he was in the presence of Fats Domino's impeccable musicians, some of whom scoffed at what they saw as his amateurism, not to mention the presence of Bumps Blackwell, a taskmaster the likes of which he hadn't encountered yet in his brief showbiz career.

Little Richard may have looked like Tarzan, says Blackwell, but he sounded like Mickey Mouse, and a listen to the first disc in the Specialty Sessions set bears this out. "Lónesome and Blue" and "All Night Long" are slow and bluesy; there are some trills and other vocal dynamics, but those sound accidental, as though the singer is trying to behave himself. Here he sounds more like B. B. King than himself, which wasn't altogether inappropriate, since Art Rupe was looking for someone to catch up with and maybe even overtake the famed bluesman. "Wonderin'" has a doowop tinge, and "She's My Star" seems to be accompanied by little more than backing vocals; were it not for the occasional tap on a snare drum, you'd think this one was sung by four hepcats on a Bronx street corner.

There are a couple of takes of "Kansas City" on the disc that suggest both the frustration and the promise of the session; an annoyed voice can be heard starting and stopping the song until finally a danceable 2' 40" version is laid down. But "Kansas City" was a cover — great song, but Specialty was looking for original songs and an original artist to deliver them. With that, the first day of recording ended in disappointment.

And the second day started the same way: "I couldn't go back to Rupe with the material," says Blackwell. So they went to lunch.

The Dew Drop Inn on Lasalle Street was a natural choice; from 1945 to 1970, it brought in top-flight black entertainers, from Ivory Joe Hunter and Clarence "Gatemouth" Brown as well as Ray Charles and James Brown, Sam Cooke, the Ike & Tina Turner Revue, Joe Tex and Otis Redding. It was a venue where Little Richard would have felt comfortable, especially considering that the MC at the Dew Drop was a transvestite named Patsy Valdeler, known as "The Toast of New Orleans" and sometimes just "Toast."

Plus Richard was "like any other ham," remembers Blackwell, so when he sees the piano at the Dew Drop Inn, he begins to bang away and sing, as the producer recalls, "Awop-bop-a-loo-mop, a-good Goddam-Tutti Frutti, good booty. . . ." It's Richard's bus-station mouth-off plus, his rebuke of a demanding boss carbonated with the heady fizz of gay Macon night life.

It would also be a hit, Blackwell realizes, only not with those words.

So he calls on the insistent Dorothy La Bostrie, who'd come by the studio to see how the recording of her song was going. At first glance, La Bostrie doesn't seem like the best choice; the song on disc one of the Specialty Sessions before the two takes of "Tutti Frutti" is La Bostrie's "I'm Just a Lonely Guy," which is more snoozy than bluesy; anyone who's ever been to a live show will recognize it instantly as the kind of number a band plays between rave-ups so it can recuperate and catch its breath.

But, hey: Lennon and McCartney made world-changing music together, though it's doubtful that either would have had a successful solo career had they not collaborated first, and the same is true for Jagger and

Richards. When it comes to teamwork, the pages in rock 'n' roll's alchemical handbook are blank, and they can only be filled in by the musicians who, and often against their will, have backed into an unholy alliance that neither fully understands.

All art is the result of the deliberate transformed by the accidental; the poet wields his words and the composer his notes obsessively, and then something happens — a chance encounter with a stranger, a snatch of overheard conversation, a dream of a long-dead friend — and the work spins off into a totally new plane. The original poem or symphony or painting or screenplay explodes and reassembles itself, taking on immortal life the way a hero does when he's wounded by the monster and heals and returns to the world a monster himself.

And "monster" is not a hastily chosen word; the literary theorist Wolfgang Iser says all art has a fundamental asymmetry, that there are always gaps that only the reader can fill in. That's the problem with art that is wholly deliberate, like bad pop songs and formula movies; there's been no accident, nothing to rough up that innocuous perfection. Back in the eighteenth century, Edmund Burke divided all art into the beautiful and the sublime, with the beautiful being smooth and pleasing, the sublime horrific and fascinating. We like the cute little girl in the Frankenstein movie, but it's the monster that we fear and dream of when we're at home in the dark and we think we hear a footstep in the other room.

So who's responsible for that part of the song that changed it all? Depends on who you listen to: according to

Bumps Blackwell, the sound of the original "Tutti Frutti" was everything he'd been looking for up to that moment; it's just that he couldn't exactly imagine the words going out over the airwaves as Dad spits out his coffee and Mom drops her spatula long enough to spin the dial and Junior is banished to his room, maybe forever.

So he brings Dorothy La Bostrie to the Dew Drop Inn. She was "so thin she looked like six o'clock," says Bumps, and "just had to close one eye and she looked like a needle." She didn't know a thing about melody, but she wrote fast and wrote clean, so Bumps told her to listen to the original words and sanitize them.

Then a twofold problem arose, which was that Richard was too embarrassed to sing his nasty song and Dorothy was reluctant to listen to anything that enthusiastically endorsed an act that the Bible was dead set against. So Bumps asked Richard if he had a grudge against money; to Dorothy, he pointed out that a husbandless woman with a houseful of kids could stand to make a little cash herself. "I talked," he says, "using every argument I could think of."

Finally, ka-ching! Bumps tells Richard to face the wall and sing "Tutti Frutti," which he does two or maybe three times while Dorothy La Bostrie listens. One can only wonder what was going through her mind.

The break over, the musicians go back to the studio and lay down "Directly From My Heart to You" and "I'm Just a Lonely Guy," leaving La Bostrie to doodle on her note pad. When you listen to these two cuts on the Specialty Sessions, you can already tell a difference, as though the raw energy of the impromptu musicale at the Dew Drop has given the music a new rough vigor. Back in Los Angeles, Art Rupe will like these, Bumps is thinking: "Those two I could have gotten by with — just by the skin of my teeth."

And then, 15 minutes before the session ends, in walks Dorothy La Bostrie and "puts these little trite lyrics in front of me. I put them in front of Richard. Richard says he ain't got no voice left. I said, 'Richard, you've *got* to sing it.'"

For better or worse, he's got to play the piano, too. Throughout the sessions, Little Richard tried to play piano on a lot of songs, but Blackwell wasn't always happy with his musicianship. (Art Rupe disagreed, saying Blackwell should have used Richard every time because "he only plays in one key, but he's good.") A New Orleans session player named Edwin Frank played on several recordings, as did James Booker, and a Melvin Dowden is listed on the session sheets.

Of course, the obvious choice as pianist would have been the best keyboard man in the room, Huey "Piano" Smith, who would go on to write "Rockin' Pneumonia" and "Sea Cruise." Smith hated Little Richard's frenetic, one-key approach: "Almost everybody plays music — hit on the piano and go 'BUNGA! BUNGA! BUNGA!'," Smith grouses in the Specialty book. "I guess since they started callin' that playin' the piano, that's when he became a pianist. But I played on the session before he became a piano player."

But the clock was ticking, and there wasn't enough

time to write an arrangement for another pianist. "Besides," says Bumps, "that wild piano was essential to the success of the song." So "I put a microphone between Richard and the piano and another inside the piano, and we started to record. It took three takes, and in 15 minutes we had it."

And that was that — well, almost. As we know, history is what gets written, not what happens, and when you have more than one writer, you get more than one story. Interviewed by Jeff Hannusch for his book *I Hear You Knockin'*, Dorothy La Bostrie remembers the genesis of "Tutti Frutti" this way:

I was listening to the radio and an announcement came on that immediately caught my attention. It said that Bumps Blackwell was looking for songwriters. Well, as soon as I heard where he was gonna be, I decided I was gonna be a songwriter. I was working as a cook for a lady and I told her that I had to quit because I was going to write a hit record. Well, she probably thought I was crazy, but that's exactly what I did. I practically broke Cosimo's door down the next day. Little Richard was sitting at the piano and it was the first time I'd ever laid eyes on him. I just asked to hear his voice and I sat down and put 'Tutti Frutti' down on paper in 15 minutes. . . . Little Richard didn't write none of 'Tutti Frutti'. I'll tell you exactly how I came to write that. I used to live on Galvez

Street, and my girlfriend and I liked to go down to the drug store and buy ice cream. One day we went in and saw this new flavor, Tutti Frutti. Right away I thought, 'Boy, that's a great idea for a song.' So I kept it in the back of my mind until I got to the studio that day.

Okay. Makes sense. After all, songs have always been composed and revised until they reach a peak of popularity by which time the troubling issues at their base have been smoothed over and prettified, as Chris Roberts shows in *Heavy Words Lightly Thrown: The Reason Behind the Rhyme*, his study of the connection between the charming nursery rhymes of our youth and the often bloody politics that underlie them.

Still, I'm officially stumped. On the one hand, I can't imagine Bumps lying about the origins of "Tutti Frutti"; on the other, Dorothy La Bostrie sounds awfully convincing — a lot of pop songs are written about subjects more evanescent than ice cream.

Whom to believe? Bumps Blackwell is dead and so is Dorothy La Bostrie. What about, let's see . . . what about Cosimo Matassa? There's no Cosimo in the New Orleans phone book, but there is a Matassa's Market on Dauphine Street in the French Quarter, so I dial the number, and a friendly voice says, "Matassa's!" I introduce myself and say I'm looking for Cosimo, and whoever's at the other end says, "Hold on, Cosimo's right here!"

So we chat a bit, and I try not to stutter, and finally I say, "So Bumps says Dorothy cleaned up Little Richard's racy lyrics, and Dorothy says she never heard anything racy, that she was writing about ice cream. Who's telling the truth?" "Both!" says Cosimo. "Now you have to understand, Dorothy's a nice lady, but she gives herself more credit than she should. See, 'Tutti Frutti' was a club song with no real end; a guy with a blue suit might walk in, and you'd put in a verse about a guy in a blue suit. So it was whatever Little Richard wanted it to be at the moment, and at that moment, it was pretty dirty."

No kidding. But then it always had been: in *Sweet Soul Music*, Peter Guralnick sets down the recollections of Phil Walden, who would go on to manage Otis Redding and found Capricorn Records, as he recalls his first encounter with Little Richard at the Macon City Auditorium. "Little Richard just destroyed me. He was doing a lot of the songs that he later recorded, but off-color, like 'Tutti Frutti.' 'Tutti frutti / Good booty / Miss Lucy is juicy / Miss Tight is all right / It ain't the ocean, it's the motion' — oh, all kinds of things. And he would wave to all the gay guys, all his 'sisters' in the audience."

As for the joyous battle cry that begins the song, Little Richard told a *Rolling Stone* interviewer in the late 1960s: "I was working at the Greyhound Bus Station in Macon, Georgia, oh my Lord, back in 1955. . . . I was washing dishes . . . at the time. I couldn't talk back to my boss man. He would bring all these pots back for me to wash, and one day I said, 'I've got to do something to stop this man bringing back all these pots back to me to wash, and I said, 'Awap bob a lup bop a wop bam boom, take 'em out!' and that's what I meant at the time." (According to Richard, "Good Golly, Miss Molly" and "Long Tall Sally" were also written in that Greyhound Bus Station kitchen, now the Macon-Bibb County Convention and Visitors Bureau.) Cosimo continues: "Now obviously Dorothy had ice cream on her mind, and that's why it didn't take her long to write that song; she left in some of Little Richard's words and took out the ones that couldn't play and put in her own words. And you get 'Tutti Frutti' outta that."

Cosimo Matassa has a clear, recognizable voice with all the earmarks of the Crescent City sound; "verse" comes out something like "voise," though with a softer edge than that Brooklynese rendering suggests. The more he talked, the more eerily familiar he sounded. Remembering the annoyed voice that starts and stops and restarts the "Kansas City" takes, I say, "Cosimo, is that your voice I hear on the Specialty Sessions?" "Aw, yeah!" he says. "I recawded him! I was the engineer!"

Cosimo had just turned 82 when I spoke to him, and he didn't sound a day older than the 29-year-old on the records. He was there. His memory was clear, and I believe him. Besides, what he says fits with what anybody who has ever created anything knows about the artistic process, especially when it involves working with other people. You remember what you remember, and over time, memories change, and often the parts that are most important are the first to go.

Because if what you did on a certain day has lasting artistic merit, that's because the work had at least one foot in the unconscious, the realm whence come bad dreams but laugh-out-loud jokes, too. Anal sex is hor-rible! At least if you don't want it done to you. And it's funny, that is, if you're laughing about it happening to someone else. There's not a threat of prison in any movie or TV show that's ever been made that doesn't contain the promise of vicious anal intercourse, something right out of Poe via the Marquis de Sade by way of our own worst fears and nightmares.

And that's the kind of stuff you might want to forget, especially if there's pressure on your memory from some new source: after a 1970 car accident, Dorothy La Bostrie moved to New York, where she distanced herself from the music business and grew closer to the church. If I were an old Christian lady trying to get right with the Lord, I wouldn't want to think about some screaming wild guy with his pants around his ankles, either.

Like Bumps Blackwell with 15 minutes left in his work day, though, I figured I'd give it one more shot, so I called all eight of the La Bostries in the New Orleans phone book. Jocelyn, Beulah, Douglas and someone listed sim-ply as "L. Labostrie" neither picked up nor had answering machines; as I wrote this book, most of the people I con-tacted for back-in-the-day information were pushing 80, at least, so sometimes modern technology didn't come into play. Paula La Bostrie's voice mailbox was full, and the man who answered at Alma La Bostrie's hung up on me. Just, bam! Right in the middle of a sentence.

Okay, I was calling around dinner time, but I'd made it clear that I was a writer, not a salesman. Had too many people like me called Alma and bugged her about Dorothy La Bostrie, or was there something about the not so magical phrase "Little Richard" that turned the gentleman at Alma La Bostrie's off? I managed to get through to the house of Juan La Bostrie and spoke to his very charming wife, who said yes, Juan was a relative and very much aware of the connection as were others. For example, whenever he went to see Dr. John in concert (aka Mac Rebennack, the colorful New Orleans singer-songwriter), the Doctor would always give Juan a shout-out and mention his famous relation. And Mrs. Juan said her husband would be glad to talk to me, though true to his heritage, he was working long hours at the New Orleans Jazz Fest, and I never got up with him.

Finally, though, I got in touch with Marks La Bostrie, Jr., a friendly and chatty 68-year-old who said, yes, he was the late Dorothy's cousin, though she was a lot older than he was, and while he was around her as a child, he doesn't remember her talking very much about her life in music or about Little Richard at all. I began to wonder if Dorothy had not, indeed, become so churchy in late life as to look back on her association with the devil's music as something she didn't even want to think about, much less refer to in conversation. And then Marks told me something both startling and weirdly apt: that Dorothy was related to the Miller family, including Percy Miller, better known as the rapper Master P and the singer-songwriter of such tender ballads as "Dope, Pussy, and Money" and "Fuck a Bitch Cuz' I'm Paid."

Poor Dorothy: had she only known what was coming,

the gay cross-dressing world of Little Richard and his ilk might have seemed more like showbiz and less like the devil's work on earth.

Because in one of those wonderful moments where the Old, Weird America and the official one converge, Master P is also the author of a self-help book, has established his own clothing line, was appointed to the board of an inner-city high school, serves as Youth Ambassador for the NAACP (a position formerly held by Bill Clinton), and, along with his son Romeo, has developed a children's cartoon called *Gee Gee The Giraffe*, a show, according to the Wikipedia article on the rapper, "is true to the duo's mission to produce positive, educational and entertaining content."

Master P: at one degree of separation from former President Clinton, he's also the author of "Watch Dees Hoes" and "Time to Check My Crackhouse." Do I detect a wink here — as Master P promotes civic virtue while rapping about blinging and slinging, do I see Dr. Mobilio shaking his devil's child at me, Doc Hudson peddling his mixture of alcohol and food coloring to the chumps, even hear Amerigo twitching to life in the Chiesa di Ognissanti in Florence as he gasps, "They named that country after *me*?"

It's America, folks, and one way or another, everybody's got to get paid.

CHAPTER 4

I've Got It

Bumps Blackwell might have thought that at first Little Richard looked like Tarzan and sounded like Mickey Mouse, but by the time "Tutti Frutti" had been cut, Lord Greystoke was at full throttle. As metaphors go, Bumps' is an apt one: an aristocrat whose parents had died in a plane crash, Tarzan was a motherless child living far from polite society. But if the jungle where he lived writhed with menace, there was friendship, too, and aid.

So when Tarzan attains his maturity, there's nobody more powerful. True, his English is substandard, and squares refer to him as the Ape Man. But Tarzan has harnessed all the force in nature that polite society lacks. And he summons it with a single roar; when the other creatures hear it, either they tremble in fear or rush to obey.

Parents, too, looked up in horror when they heard that voice cry "A-wop-bop-a-loo-mop, a-lop-bam-boom!," just as teenagers rushed to the dance floor. That's where the real race-mixing that everyone was afraid of occurred: it was on the dance floor, and not just in the music, that the races really came together. In his biography of Fats Domino, Rick Coleman recounts incidents ranging from the ridiculous to the sublime, an example of the former being the 1956 show in Houston where blacks were allowed to dance but not whites, though when white teenagers hit the dance floor, it was decided that only whites could dance. "I won't play if Negroes can't dance," said Domino in a rare outspoken moment, though when teens of every shade began to bop together, police stopped the show, provoking a riot.

On a happier occasion, the sheriff in a Mississippi town tried to put back up a rope that segregated dancers had knocked down, but the mayor stopped him, saying, "Everybody here knows each other." In a mirror image of this scene, Buddy Holly and the Crickets were booked into the Apollo Theatre in 1957 by a promoter who assumed they were a black group. They won over the audience anyway, though not initially, as portrayed in the 1978 movie *The Buddy Holly Story*; they were booed their first time on stage and needed to perform twice more before the applause came. Later, rock impresario Bill Graham introduced audiences at the Fillmore and the Fillmore West to such white groups as Jefferson Airplane, Janis Joplin and the Grateful Dead, but also to artists like Otis Redding, Chuck Berry and Santana, often on the same stage.

And it all started with a single work of genius. "Tutti

Frutti" was "exciting enough to get played on white pop music stations," according to *The Rolling Stone Illustrated History of Rock & Roll*, "innocuous enough to prevent it from getting banned. For youngsters who had never heard black performers singing at full throttle, the effect was hypnotizing. Even though the words had been cleaned up, the song's pure sexual excitement came through as plain as day. . . . Parents who might well tolerate Elvis Presley balked at the prospect of having Little Richard on the family phonograph. Yet the record soon sold 500,000 copies and had an impact far beyond its sales, [for] Richard succeeded in building strong ties to an audience that included hordes of white as well as black kids."

Grace Lichtenstein and Laura Dankner call the song that rose to #2 on the Billboard rhythm 'n' blues chart "a cannon shot among the first volleys that heralded a new age, a 150-proof nonsense song that distilled the essence of rock 'n' roll." But it's also a civil rights document as much as the Brown v. Board of Education ruling or the speeches of Martin Luther King.

To parents and kids alike, though, the main thing about Little Richard's sound was that it was so primal. But sometimes it takes a lot of artistry to create a primitive sound. There are many versions of how the Tarzan cry in the movies evolved. A typical one comes from MGM film editor Tom Held, who claimed that the yell was a combination of many different sound tracks laid upon one another: actor Johnny Weismuller's voice, the howl of a hyena, the bleat of a camel, the growl of a dog and the plucked sound of a violin G-string.

Little Richard's sound, too, is not the same at the beginning of the Specialty Sessions as it is later. At first, it's a reedy, trilling tenor with an occasional lisp — what Mickey Mouse would sound like if he had a pompadour and wore Pancake 31 makeup, say. A song like "Maybe I'm Right" is soporific; you can almost see the slow dancers rock from side to side, the chaperone rushing over to slap the boy's hands as they slide down over the girl's fanny. From time to time, you can hear Little Richard say "Thank you" for one reason or another, as though he's more eager to please than to be himself.

"Directly From My Heart" is a little gutsier, as though the singer is feeling a little bolder, maybe a little more aware of what the producer wants him to do. The same is true with "Baby": if you heard it and didn't know who was singing, you'd say, "This guy sounds like Little Richard — well, sort of." By the time the musicians get to "I'm Just a Lonely Guy (All Alone)," the voice is there, raspy and loud, but the lyrics are lame. This is a Dorothy La Bostrie song, and nothing about the words suggests that she's worth a callback. One can almost sense Bumps's desperation at the end of the day when 15 minutes remained on the clock and the only rewrite man was a skinny gal with ice cream on her mind. Tarzan's thumping his chest, but the sounds that are coming out of his mouth are still too civilized.

Frustrated artists know there's only one thing to do when the art's not coming, and that's to take a break. Which is what happened: the next two cuts on disc one of the Specialty Sessions are "Tutti Frutti," take two and then the master. The cuts are not that different (there's only a two-second difference in length), though the master is slightly more idiomatic; you don't know what the gal named Daisy *does* to the singer in take two, for instance, whereas you don't know what she *do* to him in the master. Sometimes, only street grammar will do. This isn't school, after all; it's rock 'n' roll, which only happens after the bell rings and the kids race down to the malt shop, the closest thing in their little town to Tarzan's tree.

By this time in the day, Little Richard is fully himself, or at least the early version of the self that he'll keep refining — coarsening, actually — for the rest of his career. The songs on this and the next two discs in the set don't evolve in a straight uphill ascent, of course, just as human evolution didn't march out of the sea and onto dry land the way it's represented in the cartoon in which a fish becomes a salamander and then a monkey and a man. The jury's still out on the exact phases of human evolution, though the arty kind looks more like the Dow Jones Industrial Average: lots of peaks and valleys but, over time, upward progress.

And it's not just the singer's voice that's changing. That alteration was key to his career, but at the same time, another change was taking place that would mark a far more significant seam in the history of popular music.

You can hear this change if you listen to the two takes of "Long Tall Sally" that were laid down on November 29, 1955 and then the one recorded just over two months later. The two initial takes aren't that different; they both begin this way: Gonna-tell-Aunt-Maaary-'bout-Uncle-John, and so on.

But the take from February 7, 1956 is the one we know today: Gonna-TELL-Aunt-MARy-'BOUT-Uncle-JOHN! That's the backbeat entering American popular music. If there are four beats in a bar of 4/4 music and you start clapping when you start singing, it makes sense for the first and third beat to be emphasized, as in the first two cuts of "Long Tall Sally." But if you skip that first beat and hit the second and fourth beats hard, as in the canonical version of the song, then you're laying down the backbeat.

The expected beat's what you hear in one of those white-bread churches or at a civic function where people don't sing very much but somehow a song is introduced — there's a guest speaker, say, who has no idea how atonal the audience is, or it's a holiday — and the next thing you know, people are singing and clapping. Only the syllables and the claps are reinforcing rather than complement-ing each other: it's GOD/clap-BLESS/clap-aMER/clap/ica, not GOD-BLESS-clap-aMERiCA-clap. The beat of official America is the expected beat, the rhythm of state-house and sanctuary, whereas the beat of the Old, Weird America, the beat of juke joints and juke boxes and jelly jars full of moonshine, is the backbeat. Think frontbeat/backbeat, like front door/back door. Robbie Robertson of the Band said he always knew when they were playing in the south, because that's where everybody claps on the backbeat. Exactly.

The backbeat comes to us through the unfailingly modest Cosimo Matassa, as so many things do that began in that era. According to Todd Mouton, the rhythm-heavy sound that came out of J & M Recording Studio is referred to as the Cosimo Sound, a tag that Matassa shrugs off. "People give me too much credit," he says, laughing. "I was rhythm-centric. What I was doing was being real careful to capture what local guys were doing. I didn't invent it, and I'm no musician, so I didn't play it. They played it, and my job was to put it down on the recording."

In a sense, Little Richard is responsible for the backbeat, at least indirectly, because his jabbing right hand piano trills meant something had to give in the rhythm section, so legendary drummer Earl Palmer shifted the beat away from the one and three and onto the two and four. In the Specialty Sessions book, Palmer is described as the first true rock 'n' roll drummer in that he used a rhythm unrelated to jazz, swing, or r 'n' b. Matassa remembers him as a time lord; he told Todd Mouton, "We were doing a session once and the thing was just a few seconds too long. And the guy says, 'Can we do it a little shorter?' And Earl Palmer figuratively wound a clock key on his foot and said 'How much shorter you want it?' [The guy] said, 'Three seconds.' Let me tell you, three seconds he took off. It was like 2:23, it came to 2:20."

On those first "Long Tall Sally" takes, a bouncy swing music rhythm takes its place alongside the guitar, bass and piano; if it were a school kid, the drum kit would definitely get high marks for playing nicely with others. On the definitive take, the drums step up the way Little

Richard jumped on the desk when the teacher stepped out of the classroom: wop-BOP-wop-BOP-BOP-BOP! The backbeat has arrived, and it's going strong 50 years later. In keeping with the handmade quality of the world from which Little Richard's music comes, Palmer, who had invented the most popular drum style in music, had little enthusiasm for it. "We didn't realize how popular that stuff was getting," he tells Tony Scherman in *Backbeat* when discussing rock 'n' roll. "What was rock 'n' roll to me? I lived in a jazz world. I was not interested in Little Richard."

We hear you, Earl. Still, it's impossible to overemphasize the importance of beat in rock 'n' roll. Dave Marsh points out that harmonic development is at the center of European classical music. Rhythmic elaboration is all but nonexistent, Marsh writes, and dissonance is more common than polyrhythm; even tempo exists in a pretty narrow range. This idea carries through the chamber music and symphonies of Old World music into the pop songs of the early twentieth century that are commonly revered as standards — the works of George Gershwin, Irving Berlin, Jerome Kern, Harold Arlen and Richard Rodgers, among others.

In other words, traditional musical education assumes that the priorities of Europe were the only possible ones. Yet "African-American and Afro-Caribbean music, which are the source elements for rock, place the focus on other elements," notes Marsh, "particularly rhythm and timbre." This is why rock 'n' roll, even when played by whites, struck early listeners as Negro music.

"But if you fight your way through the preconceptions and begin to look through the other end of the telescope, an interesting thing happens," according to Marsh. He quotes fellow rock critic Robert Palmer: "'My feeling is that if you want to listen to something primitive, you should listen to Mozart. Because if you hear Mozart, there's almost no rhythmic variation in it, it's 1-2-3-4 forever. No cross-rhythms or polyrhythms to speak of. The way the music's interpreted, all of the tonal qualities of the instruments tend to be very clean and pristine. There's no kind of textural variety like you would get in the blues, in terms of roughing the texture out on certain words, playing around with the pitch on certain words. Nothing like that in Mozart.'"

In Marshian terms, then, we may say that, in"Tutti Frutti," the primitive musical priorities of the Greystoke clan are upended and replaced by the sophisticated rhythms of Tarzan's jungle.

Raisins are the best part of a cake, said Montaigne, but they are not as good as a cake. In the language of rock 'n' roll, we may say that the beat is the best part of a song, but a great beat is not as good as a great song. Sure, if you set the first ten names in the phone book to a danceable rhythm, people will get up off of that thing and take the floor. But they won't stay there unless the whole song cashes the check that the beat's just written.

How do unforgettable songs get written, anyway? Jerome Kern said, "Stay uncommercial. There's a lot of money in it." Kern did okay by himself when he added

"Ol' Man River," "The Way You Look Tonight" and several hundred others to the American songbook.

And when he said that songwriters should be uncommercial, he meant that most music is formulaic, so a savvy artist will startle his audience by throwing out the rules and coming up with something new, astonishing, and, once the public gets over its initial shock, addictively good.

Something like "Tutti Frutti," in other words.

Other than that, we don't know that much about how art is produced. Jimi Hendrix is reported to have said, "Learn everything, forget everything, and play," but that doesn't explain how young men and women barely out of their teens write songs of deep yearning and profound understanding of the human condition. The best recent book on songwriting is Will Hodgkinson's *Song Man*, in which the author goes around asking established artists for their rules. Or tries to: since he couldn't interview the late George Harrison, who ostensibly wrote "Something" for then-wife Pattie Boyd (though Harrison is on record as saying "Everybody presumed I wrote 'Something' about Pattie, but actually when I wrote it I was thinking of Ray Charles"), he goes to the muse herself.

Boyd isn't much help, and Hodgkinson concludes that "Something" is poignant precisely because "it is vague. A muse escapes definition, and George doesn't pinpoint anything about Pattie Boyd; as the title suggests, his fixation on her is based on nothing more than something." Still, he can't help but be dissatisfied at so early a stage in his quest, though when he vents his frustration to a co-worker, she tells him, "George Harrison's song is about something in the way she moves. ... Never does he sing about 'something in the way she deconstructs post-modernist theory and underlines a new approach towards moral relativism.'" So much for the academic approach.

The problem is that there is a hidden curriculum of songwriting that works something like this: yes, there are rules, but nobody knows what they are, and nobody can explain how you learn them — not even Art Rupe, with his stopwatch and metronome, analyzing "race records" like an alchemist in search of the Universal Solvent. The best Hodgkinson's interview subjects can come up with are stories that illustrate one isolated point or another. Andrew Lloyd Webber says that initially "Do-Re-Mi" went "Do *is* a deer, a female deer, Re *is* a drop of golden sun," etc., and it wasn't until someone told Richard Rodgers to drop the verb that the song became what it is today. ("Very often somebody else will suggest the slightest alteration to your song that actually changes everything," notes Sir Andrew.)

Earlier I mentioned Ray Davies of the Kinks telling of the moment he was liberated as a songwriter, which is when he listens to a live recording of John Lee Hooker's "Tupelo, Mississippi" and hears a car horn in the background, realizing then that songs had imperfections in them because they were made by imperfect people — like himself, say. "It's actually impossible to tell someone how to write a song," Davies says; "doing it is the key. We all pick up our own methods along the way." There are only 12 notes, after all. As Hodgkinson says, "even John Coltrane failed to discover the key of H."

I've said that art results when the deliberate is transformed by the accidental, but at times, it seems as though the accident is more important than what's planned. Consider this: it's 1958, say, and Jerry Leiber is making tea in his Washington Square duplex, listening to Mike Stoller fooling around on the piano and then yelling "Take out the papers and the trash," to which Stoller instantly replies, "Or you don't get no spending cash!" Within 15 minutes, Ken Emerson writes in *Something Magic in the Air*, the legendary songwriting duo finishes "Yakety-Yak" for the Coasters, a song which becomes their fourth #1 single on the pop chart.

Now if you tell friends today that you're getting ready to play "Yakety-Yak" or "Along Came Jones" or "Poison Ivy" or any other Leiber-Stoller song that the Coasters recorded, they might look at you as though you've just announced you're going to have a hula hoop contest in their living room. But the songs are as catchy and funny now as they were then. "During recording sessions," said Stoller, "we'd be falling on the floor — all of us — and staggering around the room holding our bellies because we were laughing so hard."

This sense of fun is apparent as well in the stops, starts, throat-clearings, curses, and sheer what-the-hell's happening moments on the Little Richard Specialty Sessions discs. Nobody ever said that creativity has to be fun, but when it is, invariably that joy carries over into the product itself.

Mainly, though, the songs I'm writing about in this section are well crafted, as are dozens of others written for other artists in the same era: "On Broadway," "Stand By Me," "Save the Last Dance for Me," "Walk On By," "Breaking Up Is Hard to Do," "Will You Love Me Tomorrow," "Do Wah Diddy Diddy," "You've Lost That Lovin' Feelin'," "(You Make Me Feel Like a) Natural Woman." Like Little Richard's best work, these songs are still around nearly 50 years later, thanks to oldies stations, movie soundtracks, commercials, a seemingly endless parade of jukebox musicals on Broadway and in London's West End, and covers by contemporary artists as diverse as Elvis Costello and the White Stripes. And so are "This Magic Moment," "The Look of Love," "Calendar Girl," "Loco-Motion," and "We Gotta Get Out of This Place" — some of which are pure confection, yeah, but when the Leader of the Pack rides off to get killed on his motorcycle and Mary Weiss of the Shangri-Las sings "'Look out! Look out! Look out!'" you can hear the terror in her voice; no matter your age, you feel in your heart a teenager's intimation of a mortality that's universal.

The songs that I've listed here all came from songwriting teams who worked out of New York's Brill Building in the late Fifties and early Sixties: Carole King and Gerry Goffin, Doc Pomus and Mort Shuman, Burt Bacharach and Hal David, Neil Sedaka and Howard Greenfield, Jeff Barry and Ellie Greenwich, Barry Mann and Cynthia Weil, and, of course, the paters familias of these duos, Jerry Leiber and Mike Stoller. As with Penniman and La Bostrie, not to mention McCartney and Lennon as well as Jagger and Richards, teamwork often strikes sparks where solo effort doesn't — in the midst of the necessary deliberateness, teamwork inevitably results in the fruitful accident.

Like "Tutti Frutti," many of the songs from the early days of rock came out of somewhere way to the left of left field. When a New York studio session with the Dixie Cups wrapped and most of the musicians had gone, the ladies began to sing in English and Creole a street ditty they'd known from childhood; a producer told everybody to grab anything they could lay their hands on and bang out the distinctive chick-chick-chick, chick-chick rhythm of "Iko Iko," and a kind of thumb piano that Jeff Barry and Ellie Greenwich had brought back from their Jamaican honeymoon provided the song's bass line.

Little Richard's best songs all came in a flash in the first year of his career as a serious recording artist — in a "purple patch," to use the phrase Elton John employed to describe to journalist David Wild the "specific time periods when great artists fall into an extended groove and release much of their finest work in a concentrated blast of pure artistic excellence." (Wild lists Sinatra's early years with Reprise, Ray Charles's entire tenure on Atlantic Records, and the Beatles during *Rubber Soul* and *Revolver* as examples.)

Learn everything, forget everything, and play. To Hendrix's lesson, we should add a fourth rule, something like this: as you play, keep listening until you hear what you need to hear. Look at the parts that make up "Tutti

Frutti": there are the bus station nonsense syllables, the randy club song lyrics, Dorothy La Bostrie's ice cream fantasy, Little Richard's too-fast piano playing, the back-beat drumming of Earl Palmer in response, the crafty hunch of Art Rupe, the patient engineering of Cosimo Matassa, the golden-eared production values of Bumps Blackwell.

"Tutti Frutti" is a handmade song, and many hands made it. True, some are more important than others: if any another singer could deliver the way Little Richard does, then we'd be listening to Pat Boone's Sunday School cover today rather than the fiery original. But everybody who was in that cramped studio on the corner of Rampart and Dumaine on September 14, 1955 needed to be there. When I think how art is made, I recall the words of one of the Oldest, Weirdest Americans, the Huey Long who was a liberator to some and a tyrant to others and who was shot dead by a deranged dentist in the capitol at Baton Rouge: "Every man a king," said Long, "and nobody wears a crown."

The literary critic Christopher Ricks once said that a person about to discuss a poem is like a father who's been approached by a young man asking for his daughter's hand in marriage. The critic will have to discuss the minutiae of the poem — meter, rhyme scheme, imagery, and so on — in the certainty that he will never be able to pinpoint the important thing, which is what makes the poem succeed, just as the skeptical parent will want to quiz the suitor on his education and prospects since he can't determine the only truth that matters, which is whether or not the young man passionately loves his intended. Similarly, the lyrics are, in a sense, the least important element of a song. They do matter, though, sometimes crucially, and are therefore worthy of consideration.

What verbal tools do our electrified prophets use as they reveal to us the secrets of our minds and hearts? Writers are always told to be concrete, to appeal to the senses, to use imagery. That's good advice. But every axiom has its equally true opposite, and if the concrete is good, then the vague must be just as valuable. In *What Good Are The Arts?*, John Carey argues that one of great literature's chief virtues is actually indistinctness, as when Shylock speaks of "a wilderness of monkeys" or Caliban of the "noises, / Sounds, and sweet airs" that fill the isle or Macbeth of the "Good things of day" versus "night's black agents." Carey praises "nonsense" language: Carroll's "the slithy toves / Did gyre and gimble in the wabe" and Dickinson's "The doom's electric moccasin" and "Like rain it sounded till it curved," though I prefer "Diadems — drop — and Doges — surrender — / Soundless as dots — on a Disc of Snow —."

So brevity, speed, directness are essential tools for both the near-sighted scholar dipping his pen in an inkwell and a leather-clad punkette with a guitar slung almost to her knees as they are for a painter like Jackson Pollock or just about any playwright except Eugene O'Neill. The creator throws down and moves on; the audience finishes the job.

I remember sitting beside my father as we tooled along in his four-hole Buick Roadmaster down one oak-hung dirt road or another in the sweltering South Louisiana heat, circa 1956, listening to whatever came on the radio. When I could, I'd steer the tuner to the black station and inevitably to a Chuck Berry or Little Richard song. Chuck Berry made a kind of sense to my Dad; Chuck is a narrative poet (think "Maybellene" or "No Particular Place to Go") and a master of sharp-edged images. Little Richard was beyond him, though. "But . . . but . . . what does that mean?" he'd sputter. I couldn't tell him then, and I doubt if I could tell him now. Inevitably, our conversations would end with him saying something along the lines of "Can't we listen to some *pretty* music?" and me dissolving in gales of laughter. Not that he'd have bought it, but what I should have said was that some artists make the most sense by making absolutely no sense at all.

Consider Bob Dylan, arguably the most enigmatic though, at the same time, the most successful songwriter of our time. Even when he's making sense, he doesn't, as a leisurely amble through *Bob Dylan: The Essential Interviews* reveals. Interviewer after baffled interviewer tries to pin him down, but Dylan prefers to gyre and gimble in the wabe. "I have an idea that it's easier to be disconnected than to be connected," says our greatest master of reinvention, which is why, after one questioner begins by noting "I don't know whether to do a serious interview or carry on in that absurdist way we talked last night," Dylan tells the simple truth when he replies, "It'll be the same thing anyway, man."

It'll be the same thing because Dylan is, like all the great songwriters, a true reincarnation of the Sibyl, that prophet or witch revered by the ancients for her powers of divination. She gained her power, of course, by *not* dealing from the top of the deck. The greatest of this sisterhood was the Sibyl of Cumae, who, as Virgil tells us, would set down her utterings on oak leaves and spread them at one of the mouths of her cave, to be picked up and read or scattered by the winds to be seen no more, whichever came first.

It's precisely this sense of indistinctness that explains why the best pop songs *can't* make sense. Take Sam Cooke's "A Change Is Gonna Come." The quintessence of Cooke's art and life, "A Change Is Gonna Come" is ostensibly a protest song he wrote during the civil rights turbulence of the early Sixties. Like all of his songs, though, the simple, three-chord arrangement and elemental lyrics — "I was born by the river in a little tent" — reveal more than they seem to at first, especially the verse where he sings, "I go to the movies / And I go downtown / Somebody keep telling me / Don't hang around." Who tells him, though? A girl? A cop? Himself? Cooke once told protégé Bobby Womack, "Bobby, if you read, your vocabulary, the way you view things in a song — it'll be like an abstract painting; every time you look back, you'll see something you didn't see before." You can listen to "A Change Is Gonna Come" a hundred times, and it'll never sound the same, because a good song is like a painting in which you see new meanings every time you look.

And then there are always those happy accidents that transform our deliberate plans into something sublime. What if there had been, not 15 minutes, but an afternoon remaining in Bumps Blackwell's short time in New Orleans? If Blackwell had had time to refine the Tarzan-like rawness out of "Tutti Frutti," would he have done so? What if Little Richard hadn't been a "bad" piano player — what if Huey "Piano" Smith had played instead, rhythmically and sonorously instead of maniacally, thus forcing Earl Palmer to slide the beat from the one-three count to the two-four? And what if a less dextrous drummer had been working that day?

What if Bumps had decided that the backbeat had no place in Little Richard's other songs? What seems like a new beat in rock is actually a familiar one in gospel. Art Rupe never comes right out and says so, but the backbeat is essential to the gospel "feel" that he remembers from the church music he overheard in his childhood, and it could have stayed right there, in his memory. As you listen to the Specialty Sessions, you hear Bumps and Cosimo and, later, in LA, Art himself moving the beat around, looking for what works and what doesn't. The so-called "fast version" of "Good Golly, Miss Molly" that was recorded on July 30, 1956 just plows ahead, totally unsyncopated; one quick hear, and you know why it's not the version we listen to today.

And what if Richard himself hadn't stepped up? It's not just Bumps and Cosimo and Art; as you listen, you hear the polite young man from Macon recede and the chest thumper who'd soon rule the world of rock grab his vine and leap out into space. Manic cries start to appear, from a simple high-spirited "I love ya!" to outright bossiness — "Play it in G! ... G!" There's even an occasional "Jesus!" and not a prayerful one, either. Yes, the saccharine voice of the first few cuts on the Specialty discs is still heard from time to time, but generally on songs that were never released.

So it's not just a matter of good songs being recorded. A persona is emerging, one that is neither the scamp who shilled for Dr. Mobilio and Doc Hudson nor the gay outlaw of Georgia's demimonde nor the gospel crooner nor the seasoned stage performer who had honed his chops on the Chitlin' Circuit but all of these and more. Ricardo Wayne Penniman became Richard Penniman became Little Richard the regional sensation and then Little Richard 2.0, the worldbeater.

It takes a while, but the others in the studio finally get it. In the handmade world of early rock 'n' roll, performers were often treated like livestock and ordered around at the behest of some know-it-all producer or engineer. But there is a remarkable reordering of priorities in the first minute of "I'll Never Let You Go (Boo Hoo Hoo Hoo)" on disc three, track 12, in which a voice from the engineering booth says, "Everybody give Richard a chance to sing. Richard is screaming at the top of his lungs out there, and it comes over the mike that way. He plays real — back him! Don't blow solos, all of you. Drums down, rhythm easy. Just sharp, but easy. Give him a chance. He's the vocalist."

A second voice interrupts to add, "Yeah, and Richard,

you go all out. You get as funky as you can." The first voice seconds that motion with the word "Vocally!," with an implied "but" before it. You get the impression that, by this time, Little Richard is always on, and while the kids like me couldn't see whatever crazy things he was doing on the studio floor, they could sure hear the vocal dynamics if the rest of the band just played "easy."

By this time, Little Richard is his own producer. "Don't forget your solo, now," he says to the drummer nine tracks later on "Bama Lama Bama Loo" and then "AAAAAAH! Just come in strong, just go strong. And while you soloin', just keep that steady rhythm just poundin' and do all your little things, just go mad, you know. Hey, wait, watch your cigarettes, brother, so we can get right on it — hold it, so we can get right on the beat. Ready! Watch your talking." One can only imagine how thrilled Art Rupe and Bumps Blackwell were to hear their protégé step in front of the mike and take over their jobs.

Meanwhile, another big change was taking place. Flamingly gay Little Richard, the child of Esquerita and sister of club queens throughout the South, was, like Shakespeare's Prince Hal, leaving the rascals of his younger days behind and entering into man's estate. And if he wasn't a manly man, if he still sported the Pancake 31 makeup and teased his tresses into a sprayed turret, at least he didn't look totally out of place next to the likes of Chuck Berry and Fats Domino.

Too, his lyrics were evolving. "Tutti Frutti" wasn't the only song to turn heterosexual. "Kansas City" is the place where, in the first takes, "they have a crazy kind of lovin'," and the singer says he's going to get him *some*. Now going to a city famous for a particular specialty with the intent of getting some sounds very Sodom and Gomorrah; if your bachelor friend announced his intention to go to San Francisco's Castro District or the Chelsea area in Lower Manhattan in search of romance, we'd know what he had in mind. By the time the master track is recorded, though, more audience-oriented minds have prevailed, and Kansas City has reverted to Leiber and Stoller's original locale where "they got some crazy little women," and now the singer says he's going to get him *one*.

The brilliance of rock lyrics is that they are indistinct enough to hint at everything. No need to get into specifics: when Little Richard tells us that "Miss Ann" is "doing somethin' no one can," he could be referring to anything from gasp-making sexual acrobatics to her recipe for double fudge chocolate chip brownies. "It ain't what you do, it's the way how you do it," says the little old man with the billy-goat cart in "I've Got It." And even more fittingly in a world where lovers seem to drop from a tree branch and disappear into the shadows as quickly as they arrive, the old gent tells us that "it ain't what you eat, it's the way how you chew it."

Hello, Tarzan! The transformation is complete: the Macon waif is now the master of his fate and the captain of his soul, at least as much as any of us is. At last, everything has come together: beat, piano-driven music, lyrics, the accidental encounter with Dorothy La Bostrie, the persistence that leads Little Richard to Art Rupe and, through him, to Bumps Blackwell. After years of dreaming, at last his showbiz career is well and truly launched.

The rest isn't just Little Richard's history but the history of pop music the world over. In Bromley, David Bowie was taking notes. In New Jersey, so was Bruce Springsteen. Up in Minnesota, Robert Zimmerman declared in his high school yearbook that his one ambition was to join Little Richard's band. Rick James, Prince, Justin Timberlake: the line goes back to one man. To these and countless others was given the template for the basic rock 'n' roll show: the high-profile lead singer begins with an up-tempo number, segues gradually into the ballads, ends with another rave-up, and encores with one or more hits, all the while slinging asides like a drunk guy pitching phony doubloons from a Mardi Gras float.

As I was finishing this book, a widely traveled friend brought me a souvenir from the Fifties that he'd found at a flea market; it is a Little Richard trading card that had been a giveaway with every pack of a particular brand of Dutch bubblegum. A few days after I finished the final draft, the first American of African descent was elected to the White House. This means a lot in the US; it means even more in the rest of the world, most of which isn't Caucasian. The rest of the world discovered that African Americans could lead in music when "Tutti Frutti" hit the air; now they know that someone with Barack Obama's background can lead, period. Obama says he has everyone from Jay-Z to Yo-Yo Ma on his iPod, but if he doesn't have "Tutti Frutti," he should add it. Little Richard opened a door for him as well.

One point I keep making throughout this book is that there is only one Little Richard — could the world stand two? Pat Boone tried to be the white version and is a laughing stock to this day. It goes without saying that Little Richard's truly *talented* imitators learned everything they could from him and then developed their own unduplicatable musical style. Take Otis Redding, for example, who mimicked Little Richard every week as he competed in Hamp Swain's talent shows at the Douglass Theatre. Or consider Bob Spitz's description of the first appearance at Liverpool's Cavern Club by four gangly and barely known young men:

> The audience stirred and half turned while [master of ceremonies] Bob Wooler crooned into an open mike: "And now, everybody, the band you've been waiting for. Direct from Hamburg" — but before he got their name out, Paul McCartney jumped the gun and, in a raw, shrill burst as the curtain swung open, hollered: "*I'm gonna tell Aunt Mary / 'bout Uncle John / he said he had the mis'ry / buthegottalotoffun....*"
>
> Oh, baby! The aimless shuffle [of the crowd] stopped dead in its tracks. The reaction of the audience was so unexpected that Wooler had failed, in the first few seconds, to take note of it. Part of the reason was the shocking explosion that shook the hall. A whomp of bass drum

accompanied each quarter note beat with terrific force. The first one struck after Paul screamed *Tell*, so that the charge ricocheted wildly off the walls. There was a second on *Mary*, and then another, then a terrible volley that had the familiar *bam-bam-bam* of a Messerschmitt wreaking all hell on a local target: an assault innocent of madness. The pounding came in rhythmic waves and once it started, it did not stop. There was nowhere to take cover on the open floor. All heads snapped forward and stared wild-eyed at the deafening ambush. The music crashing around them was discernibly a species of rock 'n roll but played unlike they had ever heard before. *Oh bab-by, yeahhhhhh / now ba-by, woooooo. . . .* It was convulsive, ugly, frightening, and visceral in the way it touched off a frenzy in the crowd.

When "the scent of freedom" that leaped out at him from the original rock 'n' roll fades into today's music, writes Dave Marsh, he turns to *The Beatles' Second Album*, the one with "Roll Over Beethoven" and "Long Tall Sally" on it, because there he finds "refuge and assurance." Will Hodgkinson would concur: writing of a time before he was born, a period when "music was just better . . . because people were still excited by the freshness of rock 'n' roll," he says "the Beatles wrote songs that always appear to have existed. Like all the best ideas, you cannot imagine a world without them." To Marsh, that music still feels "fresh and alive," but "not in a nostalgic sense, because when it plays, the atmosphere it creates reminds me not only that the past isn't even past, as William Faulkner said, but also that the past is more than a hint of the future, it is the passkey to reaching it."

The same is true for me and "Tutti Frutti." Marsh says "anyone who tells you there is a single greatest rock 'n' roll record either doesn't know enough to make the claim or doesn't love rock 'n' roll enough to be worth listening to." I disagree. There is a single greatest rock record, and this is it. "Tutti Frutti" makes "a breach in the known world," as Greil Marcus says of the blues. Marcus also writes that those who heard the first blues said "they'd never heard anything like this before, and they weren't sure they ever wanted to hear anything like it again" — a sure sign that a seam is being welded across the face of history. Suddenly, blacks who were merely seen were being heard. In 1954, the year before the record was released, the Supreme Court ruled that school segregation was unconstitutional in the Brown v. Board of Education case. In that same year, Elvis desegregated music when he covered Arthur "Big Boy" Crudup's "That's All Right Mama"; the white boy sang the black song with true r 'n' b feeling and gave Sun Records owner Sam Phillips the crossover hit he and the world wanted. In 1955, Little Richard made us all black for 2 minutes and 25 seconds with a song that was loud, fast, and, in comparison to Elvis's café au lait crooning, so black as to be scary.

In *Mystery Train*, Greil Marcus identifies four paradigm-breaking songs that changed the musical world: the Orioles' "It's Too Soon to Know," Elvis's cover of "That's All Right Mama," Aretha Franklin's "I Never Loved a Man (The Way I Love You)" and Nirvana's "Smells Like Teen Spirit." "Tutti Frutti" is so much more "stylistically confusing and emotionally undeniable" than these, to use Marcus's criteria; it's a supernova in comparison with his four bright but smaller stars. If genius is childhood recaptured at will, as Baudelaire said, then Little Richard is a genius in the same way that few others are. In our culture, only a handful of artists have the ability to appeal to child and adult alike; that is, to actual children as well as the child who is still alive in the adult's heart. Shakespeare, Mozart, Dickens, Twain, Van Gogh: you can gasp in wonder at their work whether you're eight or 80, just as, no matter how old you are, you'll leap or hobble to the dance floor when "Tutti Frutti" comes on.

The songs that came out of Cosimo Matassa's studio on the corner of Dauphine and Rampart Streets in New Orleans are, for the most part, what Matassa calls "celebration songs." He tells Todd Mouton that while songs like "Tutti Frutti" as well as Huey "Piano" Smith & The Clowns' "Don't You Just Know It," Jessie Hill's "Ooh Poo Pah Doo" and Sugar Boy Crawford's "Jock-A-Mo" feature phonetic vocalizations some might call nonsense lyrics, in each case the artist is using his own language to express the simple pleasures of living. "You can imagine children or adults dancing and skipping, finger-popping," says Matassa. "All of 'em move — that's the central thing with all of those songs. Some of 'em are totally child-like, but they were expressions of joy. These were expressions of emotion; you can't reject those. They get too analytical about the records. And most stuff isn't that cerebral — it's visceral."

But to say a song is "child-like" is not to say it's trivial, and to say an art work is fun doesn't mean that it can't be serious as well. A year after Little Richard co-wrote and recorded "Tutti Frutti" in New Orleans, Allen Ginsberg wrote his masterpiece "America" in Berkeley. Here the "queer Jewish commie anarchist dope fiend," as Greil Marcus calls him in *Mystery Train*, "refuses the internal exile his country has offered him," just as the gay black crippled anarchist dope fiend does the same. Everything that Marcus says about Ginsberg's poem can be said about Richard's song: each "can be read alongside the Declaration of Independence" because each is "a declaration that each American must in one way or another declare independence from America, without having to surrender the slightest connection to it, before he or she can fully and freely join it." Like Ginsberg, Little Richard "takes you off your feet and away from anything like home, makes home unrecognizable, unwanted, and then leads you back."

Wow. Think about it: a gay black cripple from a town nobody ever heard of not only changes his own life with a paean to heinie poking but also revolutionizes pop culture the world over and emerges as a cultural icon on the scale of the Founding Fathers. What a career!

And then, like that, it's over.

CHAPTER 5

All Around the World

Little Richard's genius lies in his invention of an "improper" style that no other musician could counterfeit.

Not that they didn't try. Little Richard's raucous style, gender-bending persona and sexually suggestive lyrics were anathema to mommas, poppas, preachers and politicians, which is why a number of his hits were tamed and re-issued by white artists, notably (and laughably) Pat Boone, whose cover of "Tutti Frutti" actually out-performed the original, rising to #12 on the Billboard pop chart as opposed to the source record's #17. But when Boone released a bowdlerized version of "Long Tall Sally," the Little Richard original outperformed it on the Billboard charts, #6 to #8. Bill Haley took on Little Richard's third major hit, "Rip It Up," but once again, the original version prevailed. All successful artists go through a period of educating their audiences and persuading them to accept a new art form, and Little

Richard was no exception; with his succeeding releases, the master didn't face the same chart competition from his pale imitators.

As with the composing of "Tutti Frutti," the story of Little Richard squelching Pat Boone with "Long Tall Sally" is part deliberate venture, part total surprise. Both the singer himself and producer Bumps Blackwell say they set out to write a song so fast that Pat Boone wouldn't be able to get his mouth around it. Their chance came when a DJ known as Honey Chile insisted that Bumps meet a teenager named Enortis Johnson who had a song for him. DJs were as gods to producers in those days, as they either pushed your record or not, so Bumps met with a scrubbed-up kid (like "one of these little sisters at a Baptist meeting," he told Charles White, "all white starched collars and everything") who presented him with what looked like toilet paper with three lines on it: "Saw Uncle John with Long Tall Sally / They saw Aunt Mary comin' / So they ducked back in the alley."

That was it: no more words, no melody at all. So Bumps brought the scrap of paper back to a reluctant Little Richard, who finally began riffing and came up with the hook, "Have some fun tonight." Richard started pounding the piano, the musicians were pulled in, everybody began to contribute, and before long, they had a song that was too fast for Pat Boone. Better than that, Little Richard used what would become his trademark "Ooooooh!" for the first time, and there was no way Pat Boone could copy that cry. Little Richard would later claim that the song was about a Sally he knew in Macon, but why couldn't it be that as well? The songwriting credit on the record still goes to "E. Johnson, R. Blackwell, and R. Penniman."

But just when he was really about to start schooling the world in what rock 'n' roll really was, Little Richard stepped away from the lectern. His early career was fiery and fast: from the time he began with Specialty on September 13, 1955 until he quit showbiz a little over two years later, Richard would record 50 songs (including alternate takes), from which Specialty would release nine singles and two albums.

Between early 1956 to the middle of 1957, virtually everything he recorded was a hit. He appeared in several movies, including *The Girl Can't Help It*, for which he sang the title track. Club dates were sellouts, and he began to tour internationally.

Flying to Australia, Richard glanced out the plane window and thought the engines were on fire; they were probably just hot, but the scare was a portent of a more apocalyptic vision. Along with Gene Vincent and Eddie Cochran, he entered the West Melbourne Stadium wearing a canary yellow suit, a red cape, and a jewel-encrusted green turban.

Typically, it was a big show: the Australian teenagers were starved for rock 'n' roll, and the wild man from Macon was ready to feed their appetite. Before long he was down to his turban and long underpants as the kids thrashed ecstatically and fought each other for the shreds of his garments; describing the scene, the Specialty Sessions book quotes a journalist who wrote that no one had ever "seen or heard such violent movement and noise."

As it was on earth, so was it also in the heavens. Little Richard looked up as "a big ball of fire came directly over the stadium about two or three hundred feet above our heads," he tells Charles White. "It shook my mind," he remembers. "It really shook my mind. I got up from the piano and said, 'This is it. I am through. I am leaving show business to go back to God.'"

The heavenly fireball was the expiring Sputnik satellite, but no earthly explanation could shake the singer's resolve. Besides, as photographer Diane Arbus asked, "what if we couldn't always tell a trick from a miracle?" A flaming star could be a lump of Soviet tin and a heads-up from God at one and the same time. Throw in the fact that a plane Little Richard was scheduled to fly in crashed a few days later, and you're looking at one rock-solid conversion.

And a costly one, too. "Here was a guy that was at the peak of his career," says Art Rupe in the Specialty book, "or getting close to it. If he would have blown his nose and I would've recorded it, I could have sold it and it would have made the charts." Little Richard left behind him a half a million dollars in cancelled bookings and a fistful of lawsuits, but what did any of this mean to a man who had regained his soul?

Earlier that year, a soft-spoken missionary named Brother Wilbur Gulley had rung Little Richard's doorbell to sell him some religious books and introduce him to some kindred spirits, like Joe Lutcher, a successful

Forties and Fifties jump-band leader who had become disillusioned with the music business and returned to the bosom of Abraham. Richard was ripe for just such an approach: he felt that racist, profiteering promoters were using him for their benefit, and he was also tired of the heavy touring demands as well as the unwelcome attentions of the Internal Revenue Service, which used an accounting method at odds with his.

So those signs and portents in the skies over Australia were just a nudge to one who was standing on the brink anyway. When he got back to the States, Little Richard wrapped up his showbiz career and, with Joe Lutcher, founded the Little Richard Evangelistic Team to minister to the needy and the faithless. He gave up caffeine and fried foods and became a vegetarian. He enrolled at Oakwood College, now Oakwood University, a historically black Seventh Day Adventist institution, in Huntsville, Alabama, with the intention of becoming ordained as an elder of the church. Each of these moves is a variation of some standard chapter in the conversion narrative, but Little Richard's next decision seems not only bizarre but even cruel. "I was afraid if I didn't marry I could go to hell," he tells Charles White. "So I decided to start looking for a wife."

In retrospect, Ernestine Campbell is a familiar type in the Little Richard story. Just out of high school, she seems like a sister of Dorothy La Bostrie and Enortis Johnson, the women behind the two hits that made his career. Of course, a wife's level of involvement is a little different from that of a co-writer, and if Ernestine couldn't change

Richard's career the way Dorothy and Enortis did, that was hardly her fault. "We had a happy marriage for a time," she recalls, "but I think from the beginning we didn't have a chance because I could not adjust to the lifestyle." The l-word doesn't mean what you'd think; the problem was that "having to share him with so many people was very hard to get used to."

In fact, Ernestine never saw Richard as gay at all: "We had normal husband-and-wife relations, definitely. That's why it was so easy for me to discount anything that anyone said to me at that time about him. If he was gay, he was very good at hiding it from me!" That's not the way the bridegroom remembers it: "I was a neglectful husband," he tells White. "A terrible husband. I wouldn't have married *me* if I'd had diamond toenails and ruby eyeballs. . . . I was gay and I wasn't concerned."

It should be made clear that being gay or godly was never an either/or proposition in Little Richard's life but a both/and one. The people who worked with him note repeatedly that he had his Bible with him constantly, even reading it between sets, and Charles White notes that "it was not unusual for participants in one of the famous after-show orgies to be waked up in the morning by an earnest Richard quoting passages from the Gospels."

The Bible is the hypocrite's favorite prop, but it was no more a "gimmick," as Ernestine Campbell called Richard's limp-wrist stage act, than the performer's sexual preference. After the elders at Oakwood College tired of his backsliding, which ranged from skipping classes and showing up on campus in an attention-grabbing yellow Cadillac to flirting with the other male students, they called him in for a whuppin' that ended in Richard's angry exit from the school and a return to secular performance. By this time, he and Ernestine had been married two and a half years, and his rediscovered flamboyance was the last straw.

Or almost: "I accepted his act," she says. "I even explained it later to people who asked me about it. I said, 'Well, you know, people have various gimmicks that they use, and if this is what it takes to draw and make money, okay. If you're going to pay to go and see him and wonder if he's gay or not, go see him. He's making money out of it.'" Not long after his return to the devil's music, Ernestine began divorce proceedings, never having realized that the gimmick in this phase of Richard's life was, in fact, herself.

The history of gimmickry in showbiz is as old as the calling itself. Traveling troupes in the Middle Ages lured audiences in with jugglers and dancers, just as Dr. Mobilio and Doc Hudson used a soulful scamp named Richard Penniman to bring their clientele to the stage. Some of the con men from the Old, Weird America hinted at an occult connection between their charms and potions and the power of Satan, and a showbiz gimmick can, indeed, seem like a deal with the devil.

Take the case of the original shock rocker, Screamin' Jay Hawkins. Before there was Alice Cooper or Iggy Pop or Sid Vicious, there was the singer with the powerful voice who emerged from a coffin onto a stage festooned with snakes, skulls and fire pots to sing such songs as his hit, "I Put a Spell on You." His shows were sensations, and tickets sold like free passes out of purgatory, but before long, he was trapped by the persona he had created.

As he told Nick Tosches: "If it were up to me, I wouldn't be Screamin' Jay Hawkins. . . . I'm sick of it, I hate it! I wanna do goddamn opera! I wanna *sing*! I wanna do *Figaro*! I wanna do 'Ave Maria!' 'The Lord's Prayer!' I wanna do real singing. I'm sick of being a monster." Poor Screamin' Jay: he did indeed have an operatic voice, as you can hear if you pull up him up on YouTube, but with his nose bone and skull staff, he looks more like Dr. Mobilio than Luciano Pavarotti.

One night in Macon, I got a compressed history of r 'n' b gimmickry when I was out making the rounds with Newt Collier, who for ten years was the trombone player for Sam and Dave. He toured the world with them, once doing 280 shows a year, and these days you can catch him on YouTube performing "I Thank You" with the soul music duo on an archived episode of *The Ed Sullivan Show*.

Newt and I were at a club called 550 Blues, and a decent band was working hard on stage, though the audience was holding back. So the girl in front of the stage hooks her thumbs in the top of her dress and pulls it down to show the boys in the band her sugar dumplings, and Newt says, "It's a gimmick," and I say, "Hmm?"

Newt tells me that Sam and Dave had a gimmick called "getting the Holy Spirit," which means they'd be working up a sweat and "rocking back and forth the way church people do" when suddenly Dave would fall out and the roadies would rush over to revive him, and just when it looks as though the show will have to be called off and everybody given their money back, Dave leaps to his feet and rushes back to his mike — "I'm a soul man, bah-bah-bah-bah-bah-bah-bah-bah-bah!"

And now Newt's saying the girl's plum cakes are a gimmick, too, that she's with the band, which turns out to be the case, because after the show I see her chatting with them in an amiable rather than a sexed-up or groupie-ish manner and then scooting behind the merch table to hawk their tee shirts, CDs and posters, all the while perching on a folding chair and making change out of a cigar box like an enterprising small businesswoman. Newt says Otis Redding told manager Phil Walden he *never* wanted to be on the bill with Sam and Dave again, because Otis couldn't dance, and he couldn't stand it when Sam and Dave would "pull out that goddamned Holy Spirit gimmick every goddamned show!"

But a gimmick doesn't necessitate elaborate choreography and rehearsal time. Some of the most primitive still work: Newt told me that sometimes when they had a soul revue at the historic Douglass Theatre, where all the great Macon musicians got their start, a guy would run up to the MC and whisper and point to the balcony, and the MC would shade his eyes with his hand and look up there, and a big grin would break out on his face, and he'd take the microphone and say, "Ladies and gentlemen, we have a very special guest this evening: Mister . . . James . . . Brown!" And the house would go dark, and there'd be a drum roll, and a pencil spot would shine down, and a guy crouching just under the balcony ledge would slowly raise a tongue depressor that had a picture of James Brown stapled to it. "It was a gimmick," Newt says, "but a good one, because it worked."

My final lesson in Showbiz Gimmickry, Macon Division came from Hamp Swain, and if anybody would know how to put one over on a crowd, Hamp would. Hamp was the first black DJ in Macon and the first DJ of any color in America to play James Brown; he actually helped produce Brown's first demo in the basement of the building that housed radio station WIBB in Macon. Hamp was also the first to play Otis Redding on the radio, and his *Teenage Party* show at the Douglass Theatre helped provide the first exposure Redding got outside of his church performances. He also established his own record label to promote local music, so it's a sure bet that many of the great musicians of that time and place wouldn't have the reputations they have today had it not been for Hamp Swain.

He was recently inducted into the Georgia Music Hall of Fame for his pioneering efforts, but before he became a showbiz legend, Hamp was involved at the lowest level, performing in and managing a band called the Hamptones and plying his trade in the juke joints of such metropolises as Havana, Florida (still a one-stoplight town today) and others in the tri-state area.

One day, Hamp and the other members of the band went by Little Richard's house to collect him before a gig in Dothan, Alabama. But there was no Little Richard. He'd left without so much as a note — he'd gone to New

Orleans, as a matter of fact, for the Specialty Records session that would yield "Tutti Frutti," launch his career, and change the world of music as we know it.

That didn't help Hamp, though. So he and the other musicians went over to the Tindall Heights housing project, as he told me, and located another young shouter of their acquaintance. "Richard's name was up on the placards in Dothan already; what else were we going to do?" That night, Hamp Swain and the Hamptones, fronted by a vocalist whose name is lost to history ("I can't come up with it"), tore the roof off a roadhouse in Dothan. "They didn't know it wasn't Little Richard," Hamp says. "Or if they did, they didn't care."

It's hard to see the abuse of Ernestine Campbell as a gimmick to make Little Richard acceptable to a Christian audience in an impish light. But even if she didn't or chose not to see him as gay, she filed for divorce after two and a half years of marriage, which coincided with his return to secular music — it's one thing to stand by your man while he's doing the Lord's work, another when he's batting for the other team.

In 1963, Little Richard toured Europe with the Beatles as his opening act. A year later, he again toured Europe with a little-known band by the name of the Rolling Stones. Also in 1964, he brought a fledgling Jimi Hendrix into his band; even though Hendrix was too independent-minded to stay with the show for long, later he said, "I want to do with my guitar what Little Richard does with his voice."

Custom-made for Vegas, Little Richard was booked into the Aladdin Hotel there for several two-week stints in 1968. He appeared on the Pat Boone and Joey Bishop television shows as well as *The Johnny Carson Show* and *The Della Reese Show* and was the subject of one of ABC TV's *Music Scene* episodes. He had already appeared in the films *Don't Knock the Rock* (1956) and *The Girl Can't Help It* (also 1956) and would have a role in the 1986 movie *Down and Out in Beverly Hills*, to the soundtrack of which he contributed "Great Gosh A'Mighty."

For all that, Little Richard had become an oldies act, capitalizing on the hits recorded during the Golden Age of his association with Specialty Records and Bumps Blackwell and before the evils of Soviet space technology derailed his perfect career. The success of "Great Gosh A'Mighty" gave him another little bump, but none of the minor hits of the Sixties, Seventies and Eighties ever rang like the anarchic anthems of the mid-Fifties.

Between the demands of the road and the identity issue that kept him from racing from rock to gospel and back again, Little Richard lacked woodshedding time. Some art forms rely on collaboration more than others, and pop music at its best is, as Freud said about dreams, overdetermined. A single ingredient can't possibly produce the rich stew that results when many cooks slice, dice, mince, and toss in a variety of components.

"Tutti Frutti" and "Long Tall Sally" are the result of a lengthy and error-prone process. They can't be copied. Pat Boone couldn't do it. Neither, for that matter, could Little Richard himself: it's embarrassing to listen to the first take of "Heebie Jeebies" on the Specialty Sessions (disc two, cut six), where, in a blatant rip-off of "Tutti Frutti," the singer begins by shouting "Wop-bop-a-leema -lama-wop-bobba-loo." The chorus of the song blatantly copies "Tutti Frutti" by repeating "heebie jeebie" in the same cadence as "tutti frutti."

It's not until the gifted songwriter John Marascalco, whose first two compositions, "Ready Teddy" and "Rip It Up," became hits for Little Richard, stepped in and rewrote "Heebie Jeebies" that it became a hit as well (you can hear it as cut 13 on the second disc). The original song is an example of an artist ripping off himself, of a gimmick gone viral; the new one opens with the manic shout "Bad luck baby put a jinx on me!" and morphs rapidly into something that doesn't resemble "Tutti Frutti" at all. Even Marascalco couldn't resist the lure of gimmickry, however; "She's Got It," which he co-wrote with Little Richard, is a flat-out copy of Richard's fizzy "He's Got It." If an artist could sue himself for plagiarism, he should have done so here.

Once a successful formula is established, the temptation to duplicate it again and again is hard to avoid, especially when the money's rolling in. Otis Redding died when he was only 26, yet already critics were complaining that he was overdoing his trademark gotta-gotta-gotta riff that thrilled live audiences but sounded hackneyed on records. And the chunka-chunka-chunk, chunk-chunk beat that Bo Diddley invented became so much a part of his story that he could do little else. Sometimes the gimmick that immortalizes an artist imprisons him as well.

In *Song Man*, Will Hodgkinson remarks how success is fatal to artistic evolution. Hodgkinson's goal was to write and record a pop hit like the ones he grooved to during rock's golden age, and one phenomenon he comes up against again and again is that so many of the Sixties and Seventies groups that he loves were not able to write exciting new songs even though they kept recording and touring. But how can you make the all-important mistakes that lead to great records when, as ex-Rolling Stones manager Andrew Loog Oldham tells Hodgkinson, "'those people don't even have to press the buttons on elevators'" any more? When your life's perfect, you've got staff to brush away those grains of sand from which oysters make pearls. Or, as Oldham observes, "'not being able to pay some chick child support is a whole different thing from not *wanting* to pay some chick child support.'"

Another aspect of Little Richard's fizzled career involves his audience. As black tastes in pop music evolved in the Sixties and Seventies, he was either involved in the church (he has continued to "repent" and return to gospel throughout his career) or capitalizing on the Fifties sound. As a result, his appeal became not only static but white in hue as the audience for his music defined itself largely as the nostalgia crowd. "I was always supported by white people," he tells Charles White. "James Brown was different from me. He was big to the black market. When he came to town, you could get ten thousand blacks. When I came to town, you could get ten thousand whites, and about ten blacks. When I would go to Madison Square Garden, I'd have about thirty-five thousand whites and about fifty blacks in the audience. In the whole place."

Ever one to find a conspiracy behind his misery, Richard continues: "See, in the South the R & B stations wouldn't play my stuff because of pressure from the preachers who hated show business and couldn't forgive me for giving up the ministry." And, "On the West Coast, especially in LA after the Watts riots, the colored DJs wouldn't play my stuff because I've always been an artist for all the people and not just the blacks." Yeah, but if your white audience is gray-haired and thick-waisted and has no interest in your new stuff, in a sense you have no audience at all.

For recorded music, that is: the live work is another matter altogether. "I couldn't get on no TV shows," laments Richard after his honeymoon with that medium had gone the way of his honeymoon with Ernestine Campbell. "I had to do it the hard way. I had to work and try to *create* the demand." Which he's still doing today. Which is why he is the most exciting live performer still in the business, regardless of whether you're white, black, young, old, or anything in between. Probably only a puzzled ex-wife would not find a Little Richard concert transcendent, but as I've gone on record as saying that the Georgia Peach could pull dead folks out of a cemetery and make them dance, I'd like to think even Ernestine Campbell would smile after a while, tap her toe, and say, "That Richard . . . he may not have been husband material, but he sure can put on a show."

Looking back at Little Richard's career — his youthful

apprenticeship in medicine shows, the handmade recording sessions at Cosimo Matassa's studio, his accidental encounter with Dorothy La Bostrie, his Dr. Jekyll/Mr. Hyde gyrations between God's music and the devil's — it's easy to think of all that as happening on another planet and, in many ways, a better one. On the one hand, it's silly to romanticize the old ways of doing things simply because they're old. Then again, as you know if you've ever traded in your old DVD player for a new one that's impossible to operate because the geeks have loaded it with too many functions, the old ways weren't necessarily bad.

In a *Rolling Stone* interview over a breakfast of waffles, guitarist Joe Walsh says that at one point "a really bad thing happened to the Eagles: somebody went and invented Pro Tools [an audio workstation platform for Mac OS and Microsoft Windows]. Digital editing. So now we can REPLACE EVERY NOTE! And so WE DO! We can replace the space between notes where there's NO MUSIC! And so WE DO! We can replace the commas BETWEEN THE WORDS! And so WE DO! Why? Because WE CAN!" The outburst concludes with Walsh dropping his forehead into his waffles.

The Italians have a saying: the perfect is the enemy of the good. Remember how scared you were the first time you saw *The Exorcist*? Remember how you felt when the camera started going up those stairs to Regan's room, where, if you were lucky, she'd be spinning her head and spitting up pea-soup concentrate instead of stabbing herself in the vagina with a bloody crucifix, all of which was done without the aid of computers? Or recall how you pulled your knees up to your chest when the shark in *Jaws* began to snap at his victim's ankles, even though you could see that the oddly immobile creature was just a mechanical device? The pioneering special effects artist Ray Harryhausen, best known for the Fighting Skeletons sequence in *Jason and the Argonauts*, used a stop-motion technique in which he shot a frame, moved his figures slightly, and shot again; computer-generated effects, says Harryhausen, make things appear "too realistic" and lacking in an essential "dream quality."

When I listen to a recent pop song layered over with too many synthetic instrument tracks and too much echo, sometimes I think, "Gee, I wonder what that would sound like without all the bells and whistles?" Conversely, when I listen to the J & M Studio versions of "Tutti Frutti" and "Long Tall Sally," I never wonder if Bumps and Cosimo would have done a better job if they had used "the most highly specified version" of Pro Tools, which, according to the Wikipedia article, "supports sample rates of up to 192 kHz and bit depths of 16 and 24 bit, opens WAV, AIFF, mp3 and SDII audio files and QuickTime video files, and features Time Code, tempo maps, automation and surround sound capabilities."

I just say, "Jesus, that fuckin' rocks!"

Who is the — or is there a — real Little Richard? In a time of celebrity worship, not even celebrities know who they are. Michelangelo seems to have stayed Michelangelo all his life; to the end, he was accepting commissions and sleeping with his apprentices and refusing to wash up because he thought cleanliness a waste of time. But Freud stopped being Freud at one point and became "Freud," a figure admired and loathed and baffling even to himself.

The photographer Robert Doisneau, who chronicled life in Paris for a period of 60 years and whose best-known photo, "Kiss by the Hotel de Ville," has hung on thousands of dorm-room walls (and now web sites), once said, "The world I tried to show was a world I would feel good in, where people would be kind, where I would find the affection that I wanted for myself. My photos were a sort of proof that such a world could exist."

And what is the equivalent world that Little Richard made? Wolfgang Schneider writes that Wagner's music provided Thomas Mann's characters with a "delighting adrenalin surge, holding the promise of flight and freedom," and quotes Mann's secretary at Princeton as saying that, when the German novelist listened to *Tristan* and the *Götterdämmerung*, "his face, normally so controlled, gradually lets go and becomes soft, mild, full of pain and joy." A surge of pain and joy, the promise of flight and freedom: what better description is possible of the world of Little Richard?

But let us take the repositioning a little further, and here I turn to Mark Edmundson's remarkable recreation of Anna Freud's explanation of her father's work to the Nazis when they questioned her in Vienna on March 22, 1938. "My father ... knows you better than you know yourself," Edmundson imagines her saying. "For years he has been writing about the hunger for the leader — your Hitler, your half-monster, half-clown — and all the others who've come before and all who will come later in his image." The father of psychoanalysis "understands how the leader brings oneness to a psyche — and a state — at odds with itself. He knows how the inner life is divided — ego battling id, prohibition battling desire, in incessant civil war — and how painful that division can be." And then, as though she somehow knew about the six-year-old boy who was dancing and singing for pennies in Macon even as Nazi tanks rolled through Vienna, Edmundson's Anna says that "the great man shows the people how to indulge their worst and most forbidden desires — and then to congratulate themselves for doing so. . . . Under the leader, inner conflict relaxes, people become unified. All of their energies flow in the same direction: they become intoxicated; get high, and stay that way."

Half-monster, half-clown, a leader can bring people together in benign ways as well. The Macon Meistersinger, the Wagner of rock 'n' roll, Little Richard is an anti-Hitler who melts racial divisions and gets people of all kinds out onto the dance floor, jiving together.

But it would be wrong to sanitize rock and make it a force for social good, to say, as Mavis Staples has, that "It's all God's music — the Devil ain't got any music." Rock does unlock the id. Writing of the effect of "Long Tall Sally" on the audience in the Cavern Club, Bob Spitz says "it was convulsive, ugly, frightening, and visceral in the way it touched off a frenzy in the crowd."

The whole point of the song contest at the heart of *Die Meistersinger von Nürnberg* is for the young knight Walther to win the hand of the beautiful Eva, and how can a song work miracles if it isn't magic?

Even when he's reachable, Little Richard can be bafflingly hard to get through to. Georgia Music Hall of Fame curator Joseph Johnson told me that when he called Little Richard once, the Georgia Peach tried to get rid of him by pretending to be his own butler. Which must be some sleight of hand peculiar to Macon; the same day that Joseph told me this story, Jessica Walden told me that her father, Alan, would thwart busybodies by answering his phone in the falsetto voice of a secretary who had no idea where Mr. Walden was.

But even if I had been able to sit down with Little Richard for a couple of days, there's no guarantee that I could locate the man behind the screen, presuming there is one. Yet everyone I talked to in Macon who knew him then and now insisted that, under the rainbow-colored clothes and Vegas hairdos and pancake makeup, there's a version of the same nice little boy who, as his cousin Willie Ruth Howard told me, would stop in the middle of a game and go make sure his momma was okay.

I spent one Macon morning riding around in a truck with the colorfully named Seaborn Jones. Like a lot of jackleg Southern boys born with a heap of natural curiosity and no trust fund to gratify it with, Seaborn has a lot of been there, done that in his history. He lived in Pittsburgh for a while and worked on the *Mister Rogers* television show; he's also a published poet with a couple of books on the market and a strong voice that's rich in images. In person, he speaks slowly and thoughtfully, maybe because he was also a certified zookeeper until an enraged skunk attacked him and he was so badly injured in a tumble to the concrete floor that he's permanently on chronic pain medication.

In 1970, Seaborn is spending his morning with a friend in a club called the Tropics that's since disappeared from downtown Macon. He glances out into the alley and who should he see in white bellbottoms and a green Edwardian shirt but Little Richard, so he pops out and introduces himself as a friend of Twigs Linden, manager of Little Richard at one point and then, claiming to have learned everything there is to know about managing from his time with the Georgia Peach, the Allman Brothers. According to Seaborn, Twigs went to jail in Albany, New York for murdering a man, though it was a frame-up; the real cause was that Twigs didn't make good on a kickback to the local grease. Later, Twigs died in a botched parachute jump, says Seaborn, ending his life in a typically colorful here's-what-really-happened way that I grew to expect from Macon storytellers.

"I'm a friend of Twigs!" says Seaborn, and after a bit of wheel-spinning and small talk, Little Richard invites Seaborn and his friend up to the fourth floor of the Hotel Dempsey. Seaborn warns Richard that his friend is "dangerous," but for some reason, that doesn't seem to raise any warning flags. In fact, when the two pals show up at Little Richard's door around 1 p.m., the friend, whom Seaborn describes as "a fist fightuh" (and here he takes his hands off the steering wheel and makes punchy fist-fighting moves), and Little Richard get along like old buddies, at least until the friend succumbs to the effects of the pint of peach brandy he drank and passes out. Clearly Little Richard knew what he was doing when he invited the friend as well: there's a lesson in human dynamics here, which is that, when you put two firecrackers together, you're either going to get twice as much explosion or else a warm fraternal sizzle.

So Seaborn and Little Richard, who's now wearing brown slacks and a dark blue flowered shirt and is as handsome as can be, according to my narrator, get to jawing and don't stop until 2:30 a.m. "His voice is so high, so tender," says Seaborn. "We talked about friends; we talked about Twigs, about Otis." And while "from time to time, he'd play the desk like a piano," Seaborn says he "was not at all taken with himself. He lived in the moment, and, mainly, he wanted to know what you thought, what you felt, what your ideas were." And if he and Seaborn talked for more than 12 hours on the fourth floor of the Hotel Dempsey while the formerly scrappy friend tossed and turned in peach-colored dreams, there must have been plenty to talk about.

I include this portrait of Little Richard here because it collides so sharply with the image of the mannered showman, the distrustful, even paranoid, entertainer who is all ego, whose trademark on-stage cry of "Shut up!" is just one brick in the firewall he has created between himself and the public that adores but also frightens and often simply bores him. What Seaborn Jones remembers and relates may just be the real Little Richard, the man behind the makeup.

Yet this is only the first half of a story whose second half not only completes the portrait and signs it with not the barnstorming showman's flourish but the modest scrawl of the off-duty Richard Penniman, the man who left Macon long before, though it seems as though he never quite got his home town out of his system. In the story's second half, it's 1993, and Little Richard has come back in triumph. After leaving in disgrace, that is: somewhere between their first encounter and this one, "he was run out of town," Seaborn tells me, because he drove into a filling station with "a naked lady" in his car.

Richard himself tells the story in the Charles White biography (only Little Richard would provide an alibi that would get him *in* trouble). "There was this lady by the name of Fanny," he says. "I used to drive her around so I could watch people having sex with her. . . . She didn't do it for money. She did it because I wanted her to do it. She wasn't very old. I used to enjoy seeing that. Well, I got put in jail for it. I went to the gas station and the gas station man reported me to the police. . . . They let me go, and I left Macon. I couldn't go back and play there no more because of that."

But now he's back after years of banishment, preparing for his welcome-home concert and staying on the top floor of the ritzy new Crowne Plaza. He is, of course, swamped by media, which means he's also cocooned by an entourage, one of whose purposes is to keep trifling folk at a distance. Somehow Seaborn gets through, though, and it's close to concert time, but Little Richard talks to Seaborn for 45 minutes about, well, anything, as long as it has to do with Macon and/or Seaborn and not himself. Take Seaborn's dog, which he got from the pound: "There ain't no dog like a Macon pound dog!" he says. Or Seaborn's job at the moment, which isn't what Little Richard thinks it should be: "My next road dates are in Florida — come to Florida with me!" Or, well, human nature, which is probably the same in Macon as it is everywhere, though Macon reminds Little Richard that there's a right way to do things and a way that's not so right: "That's what's wrong with the world today! People don't respect and hug each other and tell each other they love each other!"

It's what Seaborn calls a typical "rolling" conversation with the master conversationalist, one that always rolls back to you. Our truck ride is coming to a halt, and as Seaborn pulls up next to my car, he says, "If I were Little Richard, I'd be saying. . . ." And then he becomes Little Richard: "How's your car?" he shouts. "You like it? You get good mileage? Your tires okay? You gonna get back to Tallahassee on those tires?"

So which is the real man, the Little Richard who praises God in church and on stage yet is not above rolling into a gas station with a "naked lady" in tow or the Richard Wayne Penniman who is only interested in other people's dogs, families, and, by proxy, at least, their vehicle safety? He's both, of course, and, as a figure central to the world he helped create, much more.

Like the Allen Ginsberg discussed in Chapter 4, the Georgia Peach demanded full citizenship in a society that didn't want to give it to him yet. Nowhere is this more clear than in the movies he started to make shortly after "Tutti Frutti" hit the air waves. 1956's *Don't Knock the Rock*, for example, is a clear attempt to figure out just what the heck this wacky rock 'n' roll is that the kids are listening — and, worse, dancing — to. In fact, the emphasis is not on listening but dancing, or how teenagers use their bodies in new and morally dangerous ways as they jive to the sounds of white musicians who sound black (or so they think) as well as real live Negroes.

The central rocker is no threat to public morals; he's Arnie Haines (played by Alan Dale), a Brylcreemed and beetle-browed crooner who looks like Bobby Darin morphing into Ed Sullivan. How Haines could have been mistaken by shocked grownups as a rock 'n' roller will baffle contemporary audiences; he sings like Rudy Vallee most of the time and Bing Crosby when he's really feeling sexy. More or less real musicians do appear in the movie, namely Bill Haley and His Comets, seven hicks in mismatched shirts playing a watered-down rockabilly. Led Zeppelin they're not.

Thanks to Bolsheviks like Haines and Haley, rock is banned in towns up and down the Atlantic Coast. Finally real-life promoter Alan Freed, playing himself, sets up a concert in aptly named Friesville with Haley; the Treniers, who are also billed as rockers but sound more like the Mills Brothers; and Dave Appell and the Applejacks, the house band for Cameo-Parkway Records, though they're still a bunch of square white guys. At last, Little Richard takes the stage and sings "Long Tall Sally" and "Tutti Frutti."

When this happens, you see what Keith Richards meant when he said "Tutti Frutti" turned the world from monochrome to Technicolor. Richard's too-brief set is tossed into the movie like a stun grenade. Even Alan Freed and Arnie Haines look on in half-smiling bewilderment; you have to wonder if the producers knew who they were casting when they signed the Macon Meistersinger. The kids are hep, though, as they throw themselves around the dance floor. Well, not "throw": they jitterbug enthusiastically but in a disciplined way, tossing and catching each other in flash moves that, by this time, swing dancers had been using for decades. *Can't Find the Rock* would be a better name for this stinker, because, except for Little Richard's incandescent few minutes, r 'n' r is totally absent. *Don't Knock the Rock* is only preparing the world for rock 'n' roll.

Also in 1956, *The Girl Can't Help It* appeared, a marginally better movie (*Don't Knock the Rock* is all but unwatchable) that not only features real actors but at least begins to treat rock 'n' roll as though it's more than just a passing fad. For one thing, Little Richard's got the title song, which he sings as Jerri Jordan (Jayne Mansfield) walks down the sidewalk and into the brownstone where she's going to meet press agent Tom Miller (Tom Ewell) who has been hired by gangster Fats Murdock (Edmond O'Brien) to turn the platinum bombshell into a chantoozy.

Mansfield swivel-hips into the building clad in a tight-fitting black dress whose top shelf is tailored to make one think of the line that Dick Cavett wrote for Jack Paar to use as he introduced the star on his TV show: "Here they are, Jayne Mansfield" (later used as the title for Raymond Strait's biography of her). As Little Richard enumerates the girl's powers — when she walks by, the beefsteak becomes well done, the bread slice turns to toast, and so on — Mansfield's sexual energy alters the landscape. The blocks the ice man's about to deliver begin to melt. A bespectacled gent is startled when the lenses of his glasses shatter in mid-ogle. Best of all, the milkman's bottles pop their caps like giant glass penises, the white juice flowing everywhere.

But just as *Don't Knock the Rock* pretended that this crazy rock 'n' roll stuff was just good clean fun, so *The Girl Can't Help It* does its best to defang rock's viral anarchy. Jerri Jordan's actually a pretty good singer, but she pretends she can't carry a tune because her real goal is to marry Tom Miller and have a ton of kids with him. Makes sense: after all, what busty, talented girl in her 20s wouldn't want to marry a drunk middle-aged square with a dye job? Oblivious to both her crush and her cleavage, Miller takes her to a club where Little Richard is playing a spirited version of "Ready Teddy." Of course it's spirited, since he's obviously lip-synching to the Specialty recording. Clearly director Frank Tashlin is making sure the Tarzan of jungle music is staying in his tree.

But with Little Richard's next number, rock 'n' roll loses its irrelevance and steps right into the heart of square culture. As he sings "She's Got It," Jerri Jordan sashays back and forth to the ladies room in another painted-on dress (a red one this time). And boy, does she ever have it. As she shimmies and Richard yells and pounds, the categories get confused. Sex is being sold both visually and musically, but so is freedom as well as pure raw power. Both song and girl say there's more to life than cotton frocks and romantic ballads and a house in the suburbs. Jerri Jordan's got it, and so does Little Richard, and you can have it, too. You don't have to be plain or straight or hold a nine-to-five job if you don't want to. Your folks may want you to be an accountant or to save yourself for marriage, but you can lose your shit, if you want to. You can be a star.

Rock 'n' roll is played for comedy here, but the gag works twice as well because the music's hot. As are a lot of the other numbers: true, the Treniers reappear singing a non-rocker called "Rockin' is Our Business" complete with minstrel-show hand waves, but Gene Vincent, Eddie Cochran, the Platters, and Fats Domino all give a taste of what's waiting just beyond the land of bow ties and bobby sox.

Vincent appears with his band the Blue Caps (in ridiculous blue caps) to sing "Be-Bop-a-Lula." In real life, sailor/songwriter Vincent was at the cusp of black/white discombobulation during the early days of rock 'n' roll. In 1955, he was recovering from a motorcycle accident at the Portsmouth, Virginia naval base when his command-ing officer, Rear Admiral Sterling S. Cook, hired him and his band for a party at the rec hall. The week before,

Admiral Cook took his wife to see Nat "King" Cole and discovered to his horror that the singer wasn't white. And now, at the party, here was Seaman Vincent shaking and throwing his limbs about as though he was still feeling the effects of his injuries and singing "Be-Bop-a-Lula" and other songs that sounded, well, black!

In the movie as well, Vincent sounds as black as a white boy can. When the song turns orgasmic and he begins shudderin' and writhin', he shakes his silly cap off, and his greasy curls fall over his face as he claws the air and screams about a gal who sounds pretty much like some gum-crackin', bra-bustin' beauty who's the soda shop equivalent of Jerri Jordan.

Eddie Cochran comes on to sing "20 Flight Rock," and he, too, is vibrating like a guy who's got his toe caught in a wall socket. But the black artists are more subdued. The Platters sing "You'll Never Know," a great song if not exactly a toe tapper, and the always smiling Fats Domino does "Blue Monday," which is more a country tune than anything else, though it's about the rock 'n' roll lifestyle (going out and getting wasted).

It's as though the filmmakers want to keep the black acts sedated, though there's nothing soporific about the three songs Little Richard sings — there's really not a single Richard song, even one of the slow ones, that can keep that ripsaw voice from suggesting that you're in the presence of a scary power.

Oddly enough, "Tutti Frutti" isn't part of the sound-track. Maybe producer and director Frank Tashlin foresaw what it would do to the symmetry of a plodding picture. After all, it and "Long Tall Sally" are about all you remember from *Don't Knock the Rock*. Certainly Little Richard singing "Tutti Frutti" would have shown up the spotlight performance in the film, which occurs when Fats Murdock the gangster sings his novelty tune "Rock Around the Rock Pile," a lament by a lovesick con.

An Academy Award winner best known for the lead role in the film noir *D. O. A.* (1950), Edmond O'Brien surely can't have ever watched himself belt out this "rock" song without wincing. He can't sing, he can't do comedy with turning it into a caricature, and as far as sexy stage presences go, he makes Bill Haley look like James Dean.

Then again, neither *Don't Knock the Rock* nor *The Girl Can't Help It* is about rock 'n' roll. Both are about promoters: the real-life Alan Freed in the first, the fictional Tom Miller in the second. This is a period of great fascination with the businessman; in fact, the archetypal *Man in the Gray Flannel Suit* came out the same year as the two "rock 'n' roll" movies.

Not coincidentally, Frank Tashlin's next film, 1957's *Will Success Spoil Rock Hunter?*, is about an advertising copy writer, this time played by Tony Randall, again pushing Jayne Mansfield on the world. The message is clear: Rebellion Sells. Or, as a teenager who suddenly realizes what's going on in *Don't Knock the Rock* says, "It's a business, just like any other business."

Okay, so rebellion sells, and rock 'n' roll is a business like any other. But the history of business is a tale of one success for a hundred failures; car or candy bar or chord sequence, people have to like it long before they buy it.

The men who made the films were interested in box office receipts and nothing else, but within the movies, they had to sell not so much the product of rock as the attitude of freedom that came with it. After all, westerns didn't sell six-guns but the sense of power that comes with owning a gun and being able to put a round in the bad guy's chest when he tries to take your gal or, worse, your livestock.

Maybe there was a method to the seeming reluctance of the filmmakers to shove Little Richard and his band of rock 'n' roll brothers down America's throat. Two songs in one movie, three in the next: it's almost as though they're getting the parents and pastors and politicians ready for the anarchy to come. According to the dubious science of homeopathy, minute amounts of a substance are given to healthy individuals that would cause disease symptoms if given in large amounts; this way, the body's natural defenses are enhanced. Maybe too big a dose of Little Richard all at once would have given the body politic/parental/pastoral a lethal case of rockin' pneumonia and boogie-woogie flu.

Besides, the one attempt to serve up the whole story is a failure. The 2000 made-for-TV biopic *Little Richard* is a fitfully amusing bomb and probably a fun watch for anyone who doesn't know anything about the star. The lead is well played by the charismatic one-name actor Leon (born Leon Robinson), who has also played David Ruffin of the Temptations and Jackie Wilson in movies. Here he is tall (at 6' 3", Leon would tower over the singer) and straight-legged as opposed to crippled; there's a limp, but it comes and goes and mainly the latter.

The big thing about this Richard Penniman, though, is that he's straight. Sure, there's some casual cross-dressing, and once he grabs a male band member in the swimsuit area, but these are passed off as high spirits. His main relationship, which takes up most of the movie, is with a certain Lucille, a goodtime gal who eventually wants Richard to marry her. The closest the film comes to saying he's gay is when he echoes God's answer to Moses in Exodus by telling her "I am what I am" and that while "part" of him wants to marry, there are "other parts."

With that, a great romance ends, but a great song results. Little Richard's "Lucille" is as searing a song of regret as the "Layla" that Eric Clapton wrote about his as-yet-unrequited love for Pattie Boyd.

The only problem is that the real Lucille was a female impersonator in Macon. In the Charles White biography, Richard describes in detail how he wrote the song about him/her well before the time that he meets and loses the fictional Lucille of the movie. True, Richard sanitizes homosexuality in his song. But by whitewashing the singer's sexuality in the film, director Robert Townsend makes him smaller than life.

As Little Richard himself is listed as the film's executive producer in the credits, one wonders whether he approved of the inaccuracies; he has gone back and forth on his own gayness, and this may have been one of the points in his life when he was in denial. Yet "executive producer" is a term that is ambiguous and often ill-defined. Frequently someone will receive executive producer credit simply because it's his or her intellectual property that's at the heart of the movie. Thus the members of the Rolling Stones are listed as executive producers of Martin Scorsese's concert film *Shine a Light* (2008) although it's clearly Scorsese's film. Besides, if Little Richard was closely involved with the making of the movie, surely he would have noticed some of its more egregious errors, such as putting the iconic J & M Studio recording of "Tutti Frutti" in 1953 instead of 1955.

As storytellers know, though, sometimes a literal error conveys a larger truth, and there is one scene in *Little Richard* that may not have occurred in life as it is portrayed in the movie, though it reveals something about the times that, no doubt, many music lovers have failed to consider. After the singer sees the flaming Sputnik rocket in the skies over Australia and rejects rock 'n' roll as the devil's music, his band finds him brooding the following morning at the end of a dock. They beg him to come back, and one points out that, after all, Little Richard invented this kind of music.

Heady thought: here is a man, barely into his 20s, who grew up hard and, overnight, found himself idolized by fans who clawed him like tigers as he pumped out a sound the world hadn't heard yet, a music so powerful that many were convinced it was Satanic while others shoveled it into themselves as though it were a drug.

A seam had been created in history; the old world was gone, yet nobody was ready to describe the world that had replaced it, even the architect who had drawn the first plans. Previously, Leon had expressed Little

Richard's thoughts mainly by mugging and leering. Here, though, you can see real confusion cross the singer's face and real longing as well. The bafflement of the movie Little Richard is genuine and heart-tugging, and it conveys how you can be in the very heart of history and not know you're there.

In reality, the scene on the dock may have played out otherwise, though the film version reveals more about the psychology of its subject than anything he himself has said about this pivotal moment in his life. But except for Leon's pop-eyed rendition of Little Richard's songs, it's one of the few scenes you want to see again. As one reviewer on the Internet Movie Database site writes, "Interesting guy, uninteresting movie."

There is one film that accurately places Little Richard in the context of American culture; ironically but perhaps fittingly, he doesn't appear in it and is only mentioned once. The film is 1978's *American Hot Wax*, which begins with a man in a plaid sports jacket and bow tie walking down a lonely Cleveland street and entering the WROL radio station. His shift as DJ is just beginning, and the first thing he sees is a stack of 45s by the turntable with a hand-lettered note on top that says "WROL DON'T PLAY LIST." With a smirk, he pulls the first record out of its sleeve, cues it up, and says, "This is Alan Freed, and this is rock 'n' roll," and then a sound familiar to us but that must have sounded like a cry from the Congo or maybe Mars hits the airwaves: "A-wop-bop-a-loo-mop, a-lop-bam-boom!"

The versatile and underrated character actor Tim

McIntire, who died at the age of 42, plays the pioneering DJ who brought rock 'n' roll to the American radio audience in the Fifties, even though he doesn't look a thing like Alan Freed. The movie has ten times as many black musicians and fans as do *Don't Knock the Rock* and *The Girl Can't Help It* combined, but for some reason, here Freed is a cocky, balding Irish guy instead of a cocky, frizzy-haired Jew.

But that's not the only act of censorship. The Architect of Rock 'n' Roll is only mentioned once, when Freed's station manager tries to get him to sign an affidavit saying he never took payments from recording companies to hype certain artists. "If you don't sign, I can't protect you!" says his hysterical boss, and Freed counters, "The only way you can protect me is if I stop playing rock 'n' roll — if I stop playing Little Richard."

The payola scandal remains a murky chapter in entertainment history. In November 1959, Congress announced that it would hold hearings on bribes to DJs. Panicked station managers across the country fired many disc jockeys, while others quit before the axe fell. Freed's career ended when he testified at the hearings that he had taken money to promote certain singers and acts.

In principle, the practice is unsavory, though some argue that payola encouraged disc jockeys to play black musicians who wouldn't have been heard otherwise, just as others say that it helped smaller labels break into a market dominated by giants. But it's obvious that the Congressional hearings were intended mainly to punish the men who played the music, to curb their power and that of the music many thought of as contributing to the rise of juvenile delinquency.

Censoring music on moral grounds is an idea that will never go away. In 1985, the Parents' Music Resource Center, led by Tipper Gore, participated in Senate hearings to promote a rating system to identify degenerate music. Like all such groups, the PMRC probably damaged their cause more than they helped it, since they identified the records that teenagers most wanted to buy in order to tap into the music's addictive power and, at the same time, piss off their parents. *American Hot Wax* makes the complex point that the business of rock isn't the all-American proposition it's portrayed as in *Don't Knock the Rock* and *The Girl Can't Help It*, and Alan Freed comes across less as a crook than as the last honest DJ, since all the other bribe-taking jocks sign the affidavit that proclaims their innocence.

Mainly, Freed comes across here as the guy he was in real life, the man who coined and popularized the phrase "rock 'n' roll" and who correctly identified and promoted its giants. Two of these, Chuck Berry and Jerry Lee Lewis, appear in the movie as part of the big concert scene that serves as its finale. IRS agents show up to confiscate the box office receipts, the show is cancelled (but not before, in an act of supreme fiction, Chuck Berry agrees to play for free), and a riot breaks out.

Then one of those unforgettable moments occurs in which a scene that appears to be a throwaway makes a point in a way that a more contrived scene could not have. As the camera pulls away from the rioting kids in front of the theater, it cuts to a guy singing in the streets, a homeless-looking character who pounds on the bottom of an upturned barrel as he sings "Tutti Frutti." The singer is hoarse and not always on key; the sound is raw, unpolished and visceral in a way that reminds viewers that the music will always come through, that no amount of cops or congressmen can stop it.

So Little Richard is effectively "disappeared" from the history of Fifties music as portrayed in *American Hot Wax* the same way he is scrubbed from the books mentioned in my introduction, such as Nik Cohn's *Awopbopaloobop Alopbamboom: The Golden Age of Rock*, which takes its title from the song that started it all but only mentions its singer sporadically.

With "Tutti Frutti," Little Richard demands full citizenship in a society that grants it to him provided he stays out of sight. Among the bonus features on the *American Hot Wax* DVD is one called "1950s Rock n Roll Hits" that includes songs by Bill Haley and His Comets, Sam Cooke, Jerry Lee Lewis, the Silhouettes, the Big Bopper, Dion and the Belmonts, and the Fleetwoods.

No Little Richard, though.

Following Richard's explosive rise and fall in the Fifties and Sixties, he emerged in later movies as no mere singer but a cultural icon. No longer a scary outsider whose presence had to be muffled for fear it would frighten away the ticket-buying public, he began to be seen as a founder of the new culture and not an anomaly. He came out of a time when a black man could be tortured and killed simply for being the wrong color. Cheated and mistreated along the way, and by himself as often as another, he not only endured but prevailed, creating a world unlike any in history, one in which we still live. All that's missing now is the recognition.

In an overdue act of poetic justice, Little Richard plays record producer Orvis Goodnight in Paul Mazursky's *Down and Out in Beverly Hills* (1986); in effect, Mazursky gives him Art Rupe's job and puts Richard at the point in the musical production line where the real money is made. Goodnight is neighbor to Barbara and Dave Whiteman (Bette Midler and Richard Dreyfuss), an unhappy upscale couple whose marriage is first challenged and then saved by Jerry Baskin (Nick Nolte), an unkempt down-and-outer whose hobo status is more honest than the Whitemans' gilded misery.

Nolte/Baskin even manages to pull a whole dystopic community together: as a foul-smelling and profane representative of the Old, Weird America, he serves up wisdom and good vibes in equal amounts, and the blacks, Iranians, Jews, Hispanics, Asians and homeless people who touch his ragged hem end up celebrating life and love together at the film's conclusion, a New Year's Eve party where Orvis Goodnight plays and sings for the happy masses.

It's not much of a movie, and Little Richard plays a distinctly minor role. The best part here is the same as the best part of the earlier movies, and that's when "Tutti Frutti" breaks out of an otherwise ho-hum soundtrack. In the midst of a damp cynicism and an even soggier moralizing, suddenly anarchy and joy flare up like a brush fire and burn away all that sober grownup glumness.

Another Mazursky movie, *The Pickle* (1993), tells the story of a director, played by Danny Aiello, who makes a movie about a gigantic space-traveling cucumber. *The Pickle* probably doesn't deserve its 4.1 rating on the Internet Movie Database, where good movie ratings begin around 7.0. But the Aiello character describes his own movie as "a rotten miserable turkey of a piece of shit movie," and *The Pickle* itself isn't a whole lot better.

In the movie-within-a-movie, cleancut Midwestern farm kids travel to the planet Cleveland, where the people dress in black Spandex and only eat meat. The president of Cleveland is Little Richard, who, like his real-life counterpart, has a godly bent as well, since he also hawks the Cleveland Bible, according to which the Lord wipes out the original human race with a nuclear bomb because Adam and Eve got in trouble with an apple, which is why He makes them meat eaters on his second try.

The movie Aiello's character directs is a disaster, and on the night of the premiere, he tries to kill himself with an overdose of pills. He survives, though, to learn that moviegoers are such morons that they flock to his film in droves and turn it into a huge success. The best premise in the movie, which is that Little Richard is secretly in charge of his own alternative universe, goes unexplored.

One of the special features on the DVD of *The Pickle* is an interview with Paul Mazursky before a studio audience in which he says he wanted to make a movie satirizing Hollywood's tendency to make bad movies. So *The Pickle* stems from a cynical promise, like *Down and Out in Beverly Hills*, just as its ending, too, is saccharine and fake. The problem is magnified by the way the interviewer deifies Mazursky, a director whose career fizzled out about this time because he seemed to be interested mainly in making crappy movies about how crappy life is in the entertainment industry. Welcome to showbiz.

In the course of the interview, Mazursky comments on a number of the actors in *The Pickle*. Little Richard, of course, goes unmentioned.

Finally, there's *Mystery, Alaska* (1999), a sweet little Cinderella story in which a small-town amateur hockey team plays the New York Rangers for a televised event. Little Richard plays himself here; he's brought in to sing the national anthem before the game starts. There's a lovely movement when the mayor, played by Colm Meaney, visits the singer in his trailer and proposes, um, a tiny variation.

The camera cuts away, and then, a few minutes later, Richard is shown singing the anthem, but at a dirge-like pace. The Rangers are shown shivering, and they get even colder when Little Richard ends our national song and starts up with the Canadian anthem, which bewilders even the citizens of Mystery but has the intended effect of pretty much freezing the New Yorkers in their tracks even as the well-acclimated Mystery athletes chortle at the invaders' discomfort.

It's a gimmick; it's trickeration at its best. And it almost works. Will the boys of Mystery prevail? Of course they won't, but they come within a point of defeating the pro team, which is a moral victory by anybody's standards. Pluck and spirit almost take the day, and if they don't, you still have to tip your hat to the (literally) glacial anthem stunt, which is small-town chicanery at its finest.

There's no road sign outside Macon proclaiming it a twin city to Mystery, but there should be.

And then, as though by magic, the old world appears again, and not the way it was, but better.

For, as *The Rolling Stone Illustrated History of Rock & Roll* notes, "during the mid-Seventies Little Richard performed in occasional club dates and oldies shows around the United States and Europe, making a virtue of *not* having his act together, babbling incoherently between songs . . . bawling out his bands for no apparent reason, and putting his audiences on edge with a variety of schizy pranks. By his own account, this was also a time in which the excessiveness of alcohol, cocaine, and other drugs nearly brought his ruin." Or, as Little Richard recalls in the Charles White biography, during an angel-dust party he and his fellow orgiasts "was crawling about on the floor like dogs, naked."

Those days are gone. But if the beauty is still on duty, as the man likes to say, so is the attitude. Who else but Little Richard can say "I want a big fat white lady to get up on the stage and dance" and get away with it? "A big fat juicy white lady — a juicy one, now! And a big fat juicy black lady, and a big fat Mexican lady, too."

Before his October 20, 2007 concert at the St. Augustine

Amphitheatre, I had been talking to Nancy, a registered nurse who, by her own estimate, has been to perhaps a dozen Little Richard shows in the last couple of years.

When the Architect of Rock 'n' Roll issued his summons for some beef on the hoof, Nancy, whom a gentleman could only describe as zaftig, took off like a shot. Within seconds she was joined on stage by another 20 women, most disappointingly slim. Through the magic of rock, though, somehow they all turned plump and juicy as they bopped and shook.

Speaking of magic, what was in the black bag that a band member placed beside the piano stool? Nancy had noticed it during previous shows and guessed that it might be emergency medical supplies. Seeing as how Little Richard had limped out on crutches, that sounded reasonable. The trouble was with his knee ("the pain never leaves!"), and in his flowing tresses and spangled blue suit, he looked like a sea god who had been clipped by a passing motorboat.

The St. Augustine Amphitheatre was built in 1965 to commemorate St. Augustine's four hundredth anniversary as our nation's oldest permanent European settlement. From 1965 to 1996, it was home to productions of *The Cross and the Sword*, which was designated Florida's official state play by the legislature. The facility lapsed into disrepair, but in 2002, St. Johns County made the decision to refurbish it.

Recently reopened, the amphitheatre has just started to book acts. A local told me that the Little Richard show was key in reviving the venue because it's one of the first acts to pass the Who Test: when someone says, "So-and-so is playing the amphitheatre," the performer fails the test if the other person says, "Who?" After five years of construction, the new facility is a beauty to sit in, with a canopy roof that fends off inclement weather yet allows you to look out on the mossy oaks of Anastasia State Park. It seats 4,500 ticket holders, and this night, it was close to full with people in their 40s and 50s, for the most part, though the demographic ranged all the way from tipsy Junior Leaguers to motorcycle mamas, Goth kids to grandpas. You approach the amphitheatre by way of landscaped walking trails that lead to and from the parking lot. Once you're inside, each comfy seat is near one of the four concession stands selling beer, wine, snacks and caffeinated products.

The latter weren't needed. Even had there been no star performer, the ten-piece Little Richard Band put on a show that would have the dead dancing, fat and juicy or not. The group was big on guitars and saxes, which made their music loud but sweet; they sounded like World War III fought with candy Howitzers.

"I am the beautiful Little Richard," said the singer as he limped to his piano, "and you can see that I am telling you the truth." He kicked off with "Good Golly, Miss Molly" and then went into "Blueberry Hill," alternating throughout between his own hits and standards by Ray Charles, Hank Williams, Bob Seger, and such less-knowns as his fellow Specialty Records artist Larry Williams ("Bony Maronie").

He only made it to the end of a couple of songs

uninterrupted by his own fizzy glee, though. Biographical bits broke through ("I was out there when there wasn't nobody!"), as well as musical preferences ("Kanye West is so beautiful! And I like 50 Cent, but I'd rather have a dollah!"), ads for merchandise ("I'll sign posters after the show, but only the big ones!") and faith testimonials ("Don't put a question mark where God has put a period!")

Little Richard's struggle between God's music and the devil's is well documented. He stuck to the sulphurous kind during the concert and saved his evangelism for his between- and during-song patter. Yet the two trends were never separated by anything other than the entertainer's jivey impulses. After an exhortation to the audience to live righteously, he sailed into a sizzling version of "I've Got a Woman," which brought to mind the assertion by Jerry Lee Lewis, another wrestler notoriously torn between the sacred and the profane, in a concert I'd heard four years earlier: "If God made somethin' better than a lady — umm! — he musta saved it for himself!"

Little Richard sang spirituals ("I Saw the Light"), country songs ("Jambalaya"), and even "The Itsy Bitsy Spider." He organized a singalong to "Tutti Frutti," correcting the audience's attempts at "A wop-bop-a-loo-mop, a lop-bam-boom!" as he shouted, "Don't mess up my song — that song took me out of the kitchen!" He made it clear that the last two syllables were "bam-boom," not "Pat Boone," whose cover of "Tutti Frutti" rose to #12 on the Billboard charts as opposed to the original's #17.

It was his non-stop conversation, both musical and

verbal, with the other musicians on stage that made the show get up and dance, though. The men in the Little Richard Band were the musical equivalent of one big fat juicy dancing gal; they watched the maestro with a mixture of adoration and forbearance as he started and stopped songs, broke off in the middle, parodied himself, and repeated himself when he did something he thought worth repeating.

As solos proved, Little Richard's sidemen were consummate players in their own right as well as smoothly meshing parts of a slick musical machine, and they even threw in Temptations-style dance steps to boot. I figured the band members would be my best shot at solving the black bag mystery, so as I waited backstage for Little Richard to sign my poster and they left the dressing room for the bus, I asked first the bass player: "Hey, what's in the black bag?" "Oh, my," he replied, and patted me on the shoulder. The trumpet player said, "Hundred dollar bills — I hope!" A sax player may have come closest to the truth when he said, "That's his personal belongings."

The closer I got to Little Richard's dressing room, the more I wanted to say something that would have meaning to him rather than the I'm-your-biggest-fan avowals he's heard thousands of times. So as the line inched forward, I whispered over and over, "Willie Ruth Howard sends her love," figuring that if I mentioned his cousin, we might have a conversation.

Sure enough: "You know Willie Ruth?" cried the astonished entertainer! I do, I said; I was interviewing her in her apartment when you called, and we spoke briefly on the phone. "Oh, yes — and you gave her some money!" Well, yeah, I thought to myself, though not as much as you wanted me to.

A security guard warned us not to take photos or touch the entertainer, but after we chatted for a moment and he signed my poster, Little Richard reached for my hand. When I put out mine, the guard stepped forward. "It's okay!" said Richard and then "Stay close to Jesus!" as he took my hand in his. "I will, Little Richard," I said, and then thought, is that a responsibility or what? Anybody can say they'll stay close to Jesus, but I'd promised Little Richard that I'd do just that.

As I left, I saw the black bag on a table. Up close, it looked a lot more ordinary than it had before. It probably did contain his personal stuff.

But what would the personal belongings of Little Richard be like? Nothing else about him is ordinary. So does the black bag contain a wallet, a comb, a toothbrush? More than likely, you'd think, the black bag contains amulets and charms, things you'd expect to find in the possession of Dr. Nobilio, the Macon soothsayer Little Richard remembered from his youth and who captivated his audiences with the devil's child, the dried-up body of a baby with claw feet and horns. After all, Son House said Robert Johnson had made a deal with the Lord of Night.

Little Richard's too godly to have signed such a pact, but outside of magic, how else explain a song that changed music forever, a singer who has gone on for more than 50 years and seems as young as yesterday? A few months after his St. Augustine appearance, he appeared on the 50th Annual Grammy Awards, along with Jerry Lee Lewis. The Killer appeared bloated, as though he were taking steroids for some medical condition or was simply reaping the harvest of a none too healthy diet. His rendition of "Great Balls of Fire" was less than fiery; his delivery was flat, his face expressionless.

By contrast, Little Richard looked as though he had just about as much of the devil in him as ever. He was in great voice, nailing all the high notes in "Good Golly, Miss Molly" as though he were a kid again. The two founding fathers were introduced by Creedence Clearwater Revival's John Fogerty, who, at 62, probably seemed ancient to, say, 18-year-old Taylor Swift, a Best New Artist nominee and, no doubt, the youngest person on stage at the Staples Center that night. As always, though, nobody seemed more like a kid than Little Richard.

The group that opened the St. Augustine show was called Falling Bones, a self-described "party band" that wisely played covers of everyone from the day *except* Little Richard: Chuck Berry, Elvis, the Stones, Johnny Cash. None of the musicians were spring chickens, but the front man repeatedly and convincingly pointed out that the drummer had just celebrated his 83rd birthday. I borrowed Nancy's binoculars and took several good long looks at him, and he didn't like a day over 79 to me.

Magic or no magic, rock 'n' roll keeps you young. Or, as Sam Phillips of Sun Records said when he first heard Howlin' Wolf sing, "this is where the soul of man never dies." Amen, brother.

Shortly after I got back from seeing Little Richard in concert, I called his cousin Willie Ruth Howard in Macon. "Willie Ruth," I begin, "this is David down in Tallahassee," but she's way ahead of me. "Oh, yes — David! How are you doing? And thank you for those photos you sent me!" (After visiting with her in Macon, I had sent her pictures of me, her, and her grandson Vincent Harrison.)

"I'm doing fine," I say, "and you're welcome. But you sound a little out of breath — is this a good time to call?"

"Oh, yes!" she says. "It's just that I just got back from my job!"

"You have a job?"

"Oh, yes — I'm a Foster Grandparent!" she says, referring to the program through which seniors serve as caregivers to children with special needs. FGs get a modest stipend, but they put in a 20-hour work week, which is no small commitment for a 77-year-old.

"Well — bless your heart! Listen, you hear from your famous cousin recently?"

Willie Ruth's reply is one I've heard variations on a hundred times in Macon. "He might be coming to town for the funeral of a cousin," she says, which, given the size and churchiness of so many Macon families, is a statement that can be probably be made about most sons and daughters of that city who happen to be living elsewhere.

If I want to see Little Richard again, I should just stand out in front of First Baptist Church on New Street the way paparazzi hang around clubs like Les Deux and Geisha House in LA.

She's delighted, though, when I tell her about the concert in St. Augustine, and she whoops with laughter when I tell her how Richard calls for the big fat juicy white ladies to get up and dance, and the big fat juicy black and Mexican ladies, too. "That's how he is! That's how he always was — always teasin' people and provokin' them!"

She asks me what he sang and says, "My favorite is when he does that one about the bird — what's that one? About the bird that's too sad to sing?" I tell her it's a Hank Williams song and think again of how much black music and country music have in common beneath the surface differences of their audiences.

We talk on for a while about this and that, and then I move in for the kill. "Well, listen, Willie Ruth. You know I'm writing this book about Richard, and I've pretty much got it done. But there are just a couple of things I need to go over with him, and I really want to get the story straight." (Deep breath.) "I think I misplaced his phone number." (Pause.) "Can you give it to me again?"

It's hard to fool a Foster Grandparent, though. Kids have tried every trick in the book already, and Willie Ruth was on to me. "I don't recall giving it to you," she says. "But I'll talk to him soon, and I'll tell him you called."

"You do that," I say. "And when I turn this book in, I'll have some time on my hands, and maybe I'll come up and see you again."

"I'd love that," she says. "*Love* it!" I bet you would, I think to myself, seeing as how you and that fast-talking cousin of yours got 88 bucks out of me the last time I dropped by.

And then I think: is this a gimmick? Am I being gamed by a 77-year-old grandma who's just pretending that she likes me? Is she going to tell Little Richard that I'm on my way so he can call in the middle of the visit and scam me out of another fistful of dead presidents?

Only one way to find out.

Sources

Whenever it was possible to cite sources within the text without interrupting the narrative, I did so. The chapter-by-chapter citations below either provide full bibliographical information for cited sources or list source materials used for background.

It should be assumed that whenever Little Richard is quoted directly and no other source is identified, his words are taken from Charles White's *The Life and Times of Little Richard: The Authorised Biography* (London: Omnibus Press, 2003), which, since it consists almost entirely of transcripts of the singer's recollections, is more an autobiography whose sections are stitched together by White's own reporting as well as his use of additional statements by members of the Penniman family and others who figured in the entertainer's career. Below are included numerous materials that weren't available to White at the time of his writing or for whatever reason went unused by him.

Two more sources that inform almost every chapter are Rob Finnis and Rick Coleman's 30-page book which accompanies the three-disc *Little Richard: The Specialty Sessions* set and the article in the June 2007 issue of *Mojo* that proclaims "Tutti Frutti" number one among the "100 Records That Changed the World."

The most thorough discography is John Garodkin's *Little Richard Special*, second edition (Praestoe, Denmark: Mjoelner Edition, 1984). And before you say, "Wait — Denmark?," remember that recently Little Richard has had a bigger profile abroad than at home; an example is the BBC interview "50 Years of Little Richard" that aired just before I completed this book, available at: http://www.bbc.co.uk/iplayer/episode/b00f9ypl/Music_Feature_50_Years_of_Little_Richard/

Introduction

Print

Belz, Carl. *The Story of Rock*, 2nd ed. New York: Oxford University Press, 1972.

Cohn, Nik. *Awopbopaloobop Alopbamboom: The Golden Age of Rock*. New York: Grove Press, 2001.

Coleman, Rick. "Little Richard — Make a Joyful Noise!" *Wavelength*, November 1984, 17.

——— *Blue Monday: Fats Domino and the Lost Dawn of Rock 'n' Roll*. New York: Da Capo, 2006.

Dawson, Jim, and Steve Propes. *What Was the First Rock 'n' Roll Record?* London: Faber & Faber, 1992.

Kirby, David. *The House of Blue Light*. Baton Rouge: Louisiana State University Press, 2000.

Lichtenstein, Grace and Laura Dankner. *Musical Gumbo: The Music of New Orleans*. New York and London: W. W. Norton, 1993.

McDonough, Jimmy. *Shakey: Neil Young's Biography*. New York: Random House, 2002.

Miller, Zell. *They Heard Georgia Singing*. Macon, GA: Mercer University Press, 1996.

Mojo, #163 (June 2007).

Nicholl, Charles. *The Lodger Shakespeare: His Life on Silver Street*. New York: Viking, 2008.

Rolling Stone, #1047 (March 6, 2008).

Studwell, William E. and D. F. Lonergan, *The Classic Rock and Roll Reader: Rock Music from Its Beginnings to the Mid-1970s*. New York, London, and Oxford: Haworth Press,1999.

Web

http://en.wikipedia.org/wiki First_rock_and_roll_record
http://www.rockabillyhall.com/JLL.html
http://www.rockhall.com/inductee/chuck-berry
http://www.rockhall.com/inductee/jerry-lee-lewis

Chapter 1: Early One Morning

Print

"In the Beginning Was the Word . . .." *Mojo*, #163 (June 2007), 90–5.

Manis, Andrew M. *Macon Black and White: An Unutterable Separation in the American Century*. Macon, GA: Mercer University Press, 2004.

Ratliff, Ben. "He's Frail, but Still Rocking and Preening." *New York Times*, January 17, 2007.

Roberts, Gene and Hank Klibanoff. *The Race Beat: The Press, the Civil Rights Struggle, and the Awakening of a Nation*. New York: Vintage, 2006.

Tosches, Nick. *Hellfire: The Jerry Lee Lewis Story*. New York: Dell, 1982.

Web

http://railga.com/Depots/macon.html
http://www.geocities.com/eskew_reeder/
http://www.georgiamusicstore.com/artist/P4765/

Chapter 2: The Ninety-Nine Names
of the Prophet

Print

Fernández-Armesto, Felipe. *Amerigo: The Man Who Gave His Name to America*. New York: Random House, 2007.

Frere-Jones, Sasha. "A Paler Shade of White: How Indie Rock Lost Its Soul." *The New Yorker*, October 22, 2007.

Friskics-Warren, Bill. "'Honeydripper' Frames the South in Transition." *The Tennessean*, February 15, 2008.

Guralnick, Peter. *Searching for Robert Johnson*. New York: Dutton, 1989.

Herbert, Bob. "Champagne and Tears." *New York Times*, August 30, 2008, A27.

Jennings, Dana. *Sing Me Back Home: Love, Death, and Country Music*. New York: Faber & Faber, 2008.

Kemp, Mark. *Dixie Lullaby: A Story of Music, Race, and New Beginnings in a New South*. Athens and London: University of Georgia Press, 2004.

Kluger, Richard. *Seizing Destiny: How America Grew From Sea to Shining Sea*. New York: Knopf, 2007.

Marcus, Greil. *Lipstick Traces: A Secret History of the Twentieth Century*. Cambridge, MA: Harvard University Press, 1990.

—— *Mystery Train: Images of America in Rock 'n' Roll*, 5th ed. New York: Plume, 2008.

—— *The Old, Weird America: The World of Bob Dylan's Basement Tapes*. New York: Picador, 2001.

—— *The Shape of Things to Come: Prophecy and the American Voice*. New York: Farrar, Straus and Giroux, 2006.

Meltzer, Richard. Interview with Jimmy McDonough in *Shakey: Neil Young's Biography*. New York: Anchor, 2003.

Smith, Harry (ed.). *Anthology of American Folk Music*. Washington, DC: Smithsonian Folkways, 1997.

Sullivan, Russell. *Rocky Marciano: The Rock of His Times*. Urbana and Chicago: University of Illinois Press, 2002.

Web

http://en.wikipedia.org/wiki/Transistor_radio

Wilson, Carl. "The Trouble With Indie Rock: It's Not Just Race. It's Class." *Slate*, October 18, 2007 (http://www.slate.com/id/2176187/).

Chapter 3: Keep A-Knockin'

Interviews

Phone conversations and e-mails with Cosimo Matassa, Keith Spera of the *New Orleans Times-Picayune*, Hamp Swain, and various members of the La Bostrie family, especially Marks La Bostrie, Jr.

Print

Danielsen, Anne. *Presence and Pleasure: The Funk Grooves of James Brown and Parliament*. Middletown, CT: Wesleyan University Press, 2006.

Guralnick, Peter. *Dream Boogie: The Triumph of Sam Cooke*. New York and Boston: Little, Brown, 2005.

—— *Sweet Soul Music: Rhythm and Blues and the Southern Dream of Freedom*. New York: HarperCollins, 1986.

Hannusch, Jeff. *I Hear You Knockin': The Sound of New Orleans*

Rhythm and Blues. Ville Platte, LA: Swallow Publications, 1985.

Roberts, Chris. *Heavy Words Lightly Thrown: The Reason Behind the Rhyme*. New York: Gotham, 2005.

Tramontana, Gianluca. "The House of Rock." *Offbeat*, #21 (May 2008). Also available online at http://offbeat.com/artman/publish/article_3056.shtml.http://offbeat.com

Web

Hannusch, Jeff. "The South's Swankiest Night Spot: The Legend of the Dew Drop Inn" (http://www.satchmo.com/ikoiko/dewdropinn.html).

http://en.wikipedia.org/wiki/Master_P

http://www.answers.com/topic/dorothy-La Bostrie?cat=entertainment

http://www.rockabillyeurope.com/references/messages/dorothy_La Bostrie.htm

Mouton, Todd. "BackTalk with Cosimo Matassa," *Offbeat* (2007); available online at http://offbeat.com/artman/publish/printer_579.shtml

Chapter 4: I've Got It

Print

Cott, Jonathan (ed.). *Bob Dylan: The Essential Interviews*. New York: Wenner Books, 2006.

DeCurtis, Anthony, and James Henke with Holly George-Warren (eds). *The Rolling Stone Illustrated History of Rock & Roll*, 3rd ed. New York: Random House, 1992.

Emerson, Ken. *Always Magic in the Air: The Bomp and Brilliance of the Brill Building Era*. New York: Penguin, 2006.

Guralnick, Peter. *Dream Boogie: The Triumph of Sam Cooke*. New York: Little, Brown, 2005.

Hodgkinson, Will. *Song Man: A Melodic Adventure, or, My Single-Minded Approach to Songwriting*. New York: Da Capo, 2008.

Lichtenstein, Grace and Laura Dankner. *Musical Gumbo: The Music of New Orleans*. New York and London: W. W. Norton, 1993.

Marsh, Dave. *The Beatles' Second Album*. New York: Rodale, 2007.

Scherman, Tony. *Backbeat: Earl Palmer's Story*. New York: Da Capo, 2000.

Spitz, Bob. *The Beatles: The Biography*. New York: Little, Brown, 2005.

Tramontana, Gianluca. "The House of Rock." *Offbeat*, #21 (May 2008). Also available online at http://offbeat.com/artman/publish/article_3056.shtml. http://offbeat.com

Wild, David. *He Is . . . I Say: How I Learned to Stop Worrying and Love Neil Diamond*. New York: Da Capo, 2008.

Web

Mouton, Todd. "BackTalk with Cosimo Matassa," *Offbeat* (2007); available online at

http://offbeat.com/artman/publish/printer_579.shtml

http://www.johncolemanburroughs.com/mag14/1482.html

Chapter 5: All Around the World

In addition to the movie roles discussed here, Little Richard has also made infrequent non-concert appearances on television: in the *Bill and Ted's Excellent Adventures* and *The Young and the Restless* episodes mentioned in the text, for example, as well as a 1994 episode of *Full House* in which Joey runs for president of the PTA; there Little Richard guest stars as Denise's uncle and performs at Joey's pre-election rally.

Interview

Phone conversations with Hamp Swain.

Print

DeCurtis, Anthony, and James Henke with Holly George-Warren (eds). *The Rolling Stone Illustrated History of Rock & Roll*, 3rd ed. New York: Random House, 1992.

Edmundson, Mark. "Freud and Anna." *The Chronicle of Higher Education*, September 21, 2008; available online at http://chronicle.com/weekly/v54/i04/04b00801.htm

Harryhausen, Ray. *Ray Harryhausen: An Animated Life*. New York: Billboard Books, 2004.

Hodgkinson, Will. *Song Man: A Melodic Adventure, or, My Single-Minded Approach to Songwriting*. New York: Da Capo, 2008.

Kehr, Dave. "The Nation; Seeing Business Through Hollywood's Lens." *New York Times*, July 14, 2002.

Marcus, Greil. *Mystery Train: Images of America in Rock 'n' Roll*, 4th ed. New York: Plume, 1997.

Marsh, Dave. *The Beatles' Second Album*. New York: Rodale, 2007.

Schneider, Wolfgang. "Mann and His Musical Demons." *Sign and Sight*, July 18, 2007; available online at http://www.signandsight.com/features/1440.html

Tosches, Nick. *Unsung Heroes of Rock 'n' Roll: The Birth of Rock in the Wild Years Before Elvis*. New York: Harmony Books, 1991.

Young, Charles M. "The Return of the Eagles." *Rolling Stone*, #1053 (May 29, 2008), 50ff.

Web

http://en.wikipedia.org/wiki/Gene_Vincent
http://en.wikipedia.org/wiki/Little_Richard

http://en.wikipedia.org/wiki/Pro_Tools
http://www.adherents.com/people/pl/Joe_Lutcher.html
http://www.history-of-rock.com/richard.htm
http://www.imdb.com/title/tt0228528/
http://www.rollingstone.com/artists/littlerichard/biography
http://www.straightdope.com/mailbag/mpayola.html
Mouton, Todd. "BackTalk with Cosimo Matassa," *Offbeat* (2007); available online at http://offbeat.com/artman/publish/printer_579.shtml

Biography

David Kirby is the Robert O. Lawton Distinguished Professor of English at Florida State University and lives in Tallahassee, Florida with his wife, the poet Barbara Hamby. Among his 30 books is *The House on Boulevard St.: New and Selected Poems*, which was a finalist for the 2007 National Book Award.

He has written on music for the *Chicago Tribune*, the *Christian Science Monitor*, the *New York Times Book Review*, *TriQuarterly*, the *Washington Post*, the *South Florida Sun-Sentinel*, *Georgia Music*, and others.

There's more information on www.davidkirby.com

Index